WELCOME TO OUR VILLAGE, PLEASE INVADE CAREFULLY

Series 1

As heard on BBC Radio

By Eddie Robson

SAMUEL FRENCH

samuelfrench.co.uk

Copyright © 2017 by Eddie Robson
All Rights Reserved

WELCOME TO OUR VILLAGE, PLEASE INVADE CAREFULLY is fully protected under the copyright laws of the British Commonwealth, including Canada, the United States of America, and all other countries of the Copyright Union. All rights, including professional and amateur stage productions, recitation, lecturing, public reading, motion picture, radio broadcasting, television and the rights of translation into foreign languages are strictly reserved.

ISBN 978-0-573-11296-6

www.samuelfrench.co.uk
www.samuelfrench.com

For Amateur Production Enquiries

United Kingdom and World Excluding North America
plays@SamuelFrench-London.co.uk
020 7255 4302/01

United States and Canada
info@SamuelFrench.com
1-866-598-8449

Each title is subject to availability from Samuel French, depending upon country of performance.

CAUTION: Professional and amateur producers are hereby warned that *WELCOME TO OUR VILLAGE, PLEASE INVADE CAREFULLY* is subject to a licensing fee. Publication of this play does not imply availability for performance. Both amateurs and professionals considering a production are strongly advised to apply to the appropriate agent before starting rehearsals, advertising, or booking a theatre. A licensing fee must be paid whether the title is presented for charity or gain and whether or not admission is charged.

The professional rights in this play are controlled by Samuel French Ltd, 24-32 Stephenson Way, London, NW1 2HD.

No one shall make any changes in this title for the purpose of production. No part of this book may be reproduced, stored in a retrieval system, or transmitted in any form, by any means, now known or yet to be invented, including mechanical, electronic, photocopying, recording, videotaping, or otherwise, without the prior written permission of the publisher. No one shall upload this title, or part of this title, to any social media websites.

The right of Eddie Robson to be identified as author of this work has been asserted in accordance with Section 77 of the Copyright, Designs and Patents Act 1988.

THINKING ABOUT PERFORMING A SHOW?

There are thousands of plays and musicals available to perform from Samuel French right now, and applying for a licence is easier and more affordable than you might think

From classic plays to brand new musicals, from monologues to epic dramas, there are shows for everyone.

Plays and musicals are protected by copyright law so if you want to perform them, the first thing you'll need is a licence. This simple process helps support the playwright by ensuring they get paid for their work, and means that you'll have the documents you need to stage the show in public.

Not all our shows are available to perform all the time, so it's important to check and apply for a licence before you start rehearsals or commit to doing the show.

LEARN MORE & FIND THOUSANDS OF SHOWS

Browse our full range of plays and musicals and find out more about how to license a show

www.samuelfrench.co.uk/perform

Talk to the friendly experts in our Licensing team for advice on choosing a show, and help with licensing

plays@samuelfrench.co.uk   020 7387 9373

Acting Editions
BORN TO PERFORM

Playscripts designed from the ground up to work the way you do in rehearsal, performance and study

---

Larger, clearer text for easier reading

Wider margins for notes

Performance features such as character and props lists, sound and lighting cues, and more

---

+ CHOOSE A SIZE AND STYLE TO SUIT YOU

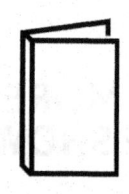

STANDARD EDITION
Our regular paperback book at our regular size

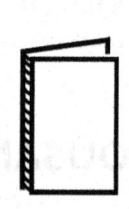

SPIRAL-BOUND EDITION
The same size as the Standard Edition, but with a sturdy, easy-to-fold, easy-to-hold spiral-bound spine

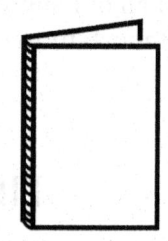

LARGE EDITION
A4 size and spiral bound, with larger text and a blank page for notes opposite every page of text. Perfect for technical and directing use

---

LEARN MORE samuelfrench.co.uk/actingeditions

ABOUT THE AUTHOR

Eddie Robson was born in York in 1978. He spent several years working mainly as a journalist and critic, producing books including *Coen Brothers* (Virgin, 2003) and *Film Noir* (Virgin, 2005), before moving into scriptwriting and prose. He wrote for BBC Radio sketch shows including *That Mitchell And Webb Sound*, *Look Away Now*, *Recorded For Training Purposes*, *Newsjack* and *Small Scenes*, as well as over twenty *Doctor Who* radio plays broadcast on BBC Radio 4 Extra and released on CD.

He created and wrote *Welcome To Our Village, Please Invade Carefully* which aired on BBC Radio between 2012 and 2014. Subsequently he has written a novel, *Tomorrow Never Knows* (Snowbooks, 2015), a stage adaptation of *Beauty And The Beast* (The Dukes Lancaster, 2015-16), several comic strips for *2000AD*, and episodes of *Hollyoaks* (Channel 4, 2014-15) and *Sarah & Duck* (CBeebies, 2015-16). He is married with two children and lives in Lancaster.

AUTHOR'S NOTE

In 2009, Ed Morrish – a BBC producer I'd worked with on a Radio 4 sketch show called *Recorded For Training Purposes* – asked if I had any ideas for a sitcom. My first attempt came to nothing, but then I came up with something called *The Resistance*.

The original inspiration was to do a sort of comedy version of the 1960s TV show *The Prisoner*: a sitcom in which the protagonists are constantly trying to escape. The village setting then developed with reference to rural *Doctor Who* (most obviously the 1971 serial "The Daemons") and Simon Nye's sitcom *How Do You Want Me?*, and I wrote a script which involved four people attempting to escape the village of Cresdon Green in the postal van of a train. As well as Katrina and Lucy, those four people included Weird Patrick, the village conspiracy theorist, and Mike, Katrina's ex-boyfriend from their schooldays. These four were the titular resistance against an alien invasion.

However, we realised it wasn't clear where the focus of the show was. There was conflict within the resistance about how to achieve their aim, but also the bigger conflict with the invaders. Furthermore, Katrina's parents had too little to do: eight regulars was way too many. We opted to focus away from the resistance: Katrina needed someone to plot with and of the other three, Lucy offered the most interesting dynamic so we kept her. Weird Patrick became a one-off character in the episode "Minimum Volume"; Mike was never heard from again.

I then wrote a second script. This one was a "premise episode" – which is what we call an opening episode of a sitcom which explains how the situation came about. So the invasion happened, Uljabaan revealed he was an alien and Katrina decided to form the resistance. However, the problem with premise episodes is it can be hard to make them funny. I was commissioned to write a third script, and everyone agreed starting with the invasion already underway was better, so that became the pilot in this book.

All this development ultimately took two years, before it found a home in a run of Radio 2 comedy pilots under the title *Welcome*

To Our Village, Please Invade Carefully. (It's not very tweetable, but it takes up a satisfyingly large amount of space in the cramped newspaper radio listings.) We got a terrific cast together and the pilot aired on 5th July 2012, which annoyingly ended up being the same day I moved house.

Radio 2 gave us a series, which I found a considerable learning curve. I'd written lots of spec scripts over the years, but this was the first time I had been asked for another four. I worked like mad on the scripts, but it proved difficult to repeat the very good response we got to the pilot. The first episode to be recorded, "Power Block", took a while to warm up in front of the audience, so we moved it to third in the broadcast order. A lot of credit goes to Ed, who tightened all the episodes up in the edit. I'm still proud of that series, but there were some gruelling lessons on the way. I've never developed more as a writer than I did across the two series of *Welcome To Our Village*.

The scripts here are as broadcast. Clearly, a degree of adaptation is needed to take them from radio to stage. Feel free to abridge these five episodes or drop some of them entirely, whether for length or practicality. There are three key locations – the Lyons's house (with several rooms), Uljabaan's house and the cricket pavilion. You may want to move some other scenes to those locations to reduce the number of sets you have to create.

John-Luke Roberts, who played the Computer, doubled up as Graham, a sort of all-purpose village idiot. Depending on the size of your company, you may wish to make use of that same doubling. The minimum cast size to perform the series as written is probably eight, with two cast doubling up as guest characters and minions (and you may need to change the gender of some guest characters). With creative rewriting, you may be able to make it work on fewer; you're welcome to try.

Uljabaan is meant to be in human guise at all times, unlike his minions. I never pinned down exactly what the Geonin look like, and this became a sort of running joke, mentioning details but never describing them. They can look however you want them to look. We used an effects mic for the minions and the Computer, and got some good cheap laughs out of silly voices. It will certainly be to the production's benefit if you can play in sound effects, as a lot of scenes rely on this.

WELCOME TO OUR VILLAGE, PLEASE INVADE CAREFULLY

CONTENTS

Pilot – "Lock-Out"

Episode 1.1 – "Taking Overs"

Episode 1.2 – "Minimum Volume"

Episode 1.3 – "Power Block"

Episode 1.4 – "Little Green Lights"

Ultimately, I'm delighted if anyone wants to perform these scripts. It's your production, do what's needed to make it the best it can be. If I can make it down there to see it, I will.

Eddie Robson, 2016

CHARACTER DESCRIPTIONS

Katrina Lyons – thirty-two/thirty-four, Katrina grew up in the Buckinghamshire village of Cresdon Green but has since moved to London, to work for an educational charity helping disadvantaged children. It's important to her to be seen to be doing the right thing – sometimes more important than getting the right thing done – and so she started the resistance against the invasion. More than anything, Katrina hates not being taken seriously.

Uljabaan – seems thirties/forties, but is an alien in human guise. Uljabaan is a warlord in the Geonin military, who are engaged in an endless war with their enemies the Thoufron. He's able to project an aristocratic surface charm, but is also quite smug and complacent. In truth he's a low achiever within the officer class, and has been posted to Earth to keep him out of the way: this is his chance to prove himself.

Margaret Lyons – early sixties. Katrina's mother. Margaret has lived in the village all her life, and effectively runs the place. Whilst the invasion isn't ideal, she can't help but feel flattered and a little excited that events of global importance are taking place on her doorstep. She doesn't really have a sense of humour and gets annoyed when things don't proceed exactly to her design.

Richard Lyons – early sixties. Katrina's father. Richard is a chartered accountant who was only a few years off retirement, and was looking forward to a quiet life, playing some cricket and maybe finishing that detective novel he's been working on. He avoids conflict where possible at home and takes the same approach to the invasion. He's warm, usually relaxed and a little diffident.

Lucy Alexander – Sixteen/eighteen. Lucy is the only child and keen to be noticed. She's joined the resistance mostly for this reason; also, all her friends live outside Credson Green and there's no internet since the village got cut off from the outside world, so she's incredibly bored. She gets stoned a lot and is regularly a beat behind the conversation.

Computer – Uljabaan's Computer runs the entire invasion scheme, on Uljabaan's orders. It speaks with an almost, but not entirely, emotionless voice. Hugely advanced, it has a personality as part of its interface and although it's not supposed to have desires and whims, it can be rather chippy. (The part could be played by an actor of any gender.)

WELCOME TO OUR VILLAGE, PLEASE INVADE CAREFULLY

Pilot – "Lock-Out"

Scene One

Int. village hall.

Effects: a meeting settling down. The meeting is chaired by **RICHARD**.

RICHARD Now, you should all have a copy of the agenda – between item nine, repairs to the fence between the playground and Colney Drive, and item ten, any other business, could you please add item nine b, the recent invasion of the village by beings from another world.

Effects: people do this. There are some tuts of irritation.

KATRINA Er, Dad?

RICHARD Yes, Katrina?

KATRINA Why item nine b?

RICHARD We can't put it after any other business because we always do any other business last. We can't do the other business, then have another piece of business.

KATRINA *(beat)* Right, I thought the direction of my query was obvious, but apparently not – I meant, why aren't we discussing the alien invasion first?

RICHARD Because minutes of the previous meeting come first.

KATRINA Who cares about the minutes of the previous meeting?

RICHARD Well Sandra does, she compiled them.

SANDRA *sniffles.*

KATRINA Sorry, Sandra, I'm sure you've done a cracking job. But recent events have not just overshadowed everything you were planning to discuss, but also everything else that's ever happened in Cresdon Green ever.

GRAHAM Actually in 1941 the village was visited by His Royal Highness Prince George, Duke of Kent.

KATRINA And did His Royal Highness Prince George, Duke of Kent erect an impenetrable force field around the village, cut off all communications in both directions, and create a mental block preventing anyone in the outside world seeing or even thinking about the village and its inhabitants?

GRAHAM No, but—

KATRINA OK, moving on.

CHRIS You're not technically supposed to be at this meeting at all, Katrina. It is a residents' meeting.

KATRINA I didn't plan to become a resident when I popped home to see Mum and Dad –

RICHARD And ask to borrow the deposit for a flat—

KATRINA To which they said no, but that's their prerogative, I'm FINE about it – but then the force field came down before I could leave, so how much more residential do you want me to be?

RICHARD *(sighs)* All right. For those of you who've been out of the loop, Cresdon Green has been invaded by aliens and sealed off from the outside world.

OLD MAN Really?

RICHARD Yes.

OLD MAN Good grief.

RICHARD So. What are we going to do about it?

Silence.

GRAHAM Do we have to do something about it?

RICHARD That's a good question.

KATRINA No it isn't.

GRAHAM Shouldn't the police do something?

CHRIS Yes, or the government, or the army...

GRAHAM The FBI dealt with this sort of thing in *The X Files*.

RICHARD They don't have any jurisdiction outside of America. It would have to be the CIA.

GRAHAM You can't trust them, Richard.

KATRINA This is all academic, as well as being largely based on things you've seen on television. The world doesn't know this has happened and we can't call anyone in. Not the police, not the army, not the FBI, not the CIA, not the BBC, QPR or REM. So it's up to us.

RICHARD What do you suggest, love?

KATRINA We could stop helping the aliens.

CHRIS I'm not helping them.

KATRINA But you're still serving them in the village shop, Chris.

CHRIS Their money's as good as anyone's. Better, in fact – it all looks brand new.

GRAHAM Be fair, Kat, it's just common politeness. They've been very nice to us so far.

KATRINA Because they want us to co-operate. You know who else co-operated with their invaders? The French.

Effects: hissed intakes of breath all round.

That's right. They want to take over the world, for God's sake – however nice and polite they seem, they're a bunch of malign, manipulative thugs who—

RICHARD *(low)* Love, you might want to calm down.

KATRINA No, Dad, this has to be said – thugs without morals, or ethics and—

RICHARD *(low)* You're being a bit rude.

ULJABAAN Richard, it's fine. I'm not offended.

KATRINA I don't care if you are. *(Beat)* Why aren't you offended?

ULJABAAN I want you to speak freely. I'm just sitting in. I'm not even here.

KATRINA Yes, you are. That's exactly the problem.

OLD MAN But he's not one of the aliens, he's Lord Ullswater.

KATRINA Yes, Lord Ullswater. The long-lost heir to Aulderley House who nobody had ever heard of until he laid claim to the place eighteen months ago.

OLD MAN What are you suggesting?

ULJABAAN She's suggesting I made it all up, which I did. I am in fact an alien in human guise. My name is Uljabaan. Anyway, carry on.

KATRINA I will.

ULJABAAN Please do.

KATRINA *(beat)* I've forgotten where I was.

ULJABAAN Thugs without morals or ethics.

KATRINA Yes – and we should stop co-operating with them. Who's with me?

Effects: uneasy mutterings.

ULJABAAN Don't hold back on my account. We appreciate we're putting you all to a lot of trouble by being here, and if you're uncomfortable about co-operating, absolutely feel free to say so.

KATRINA Um. Yes. So, who's with me?

Effects: others say "er...yes, all right" etc.

RICHARD Motion more or less carried...is that all right?

ULJABAAN Of course, Richard.

KATRINA Good.

RICHARD So, item two...siting of the new bus stop on Park Crescent.

GRAHAM Ah, now *that* is a bloody disgrace.

Effects: chorus of "hear, hear" from attendees.

Scene Two

Int. shop.

Effects: shop doorbell. One of ULJABAAN's *minions enters.*

CHRIS Morning sir.

MINION *(gutteral alien language)*

CHRIS What can I do you for?

MINION *(gutteral alien language)*

CHRIS You're sure you don't want the low tar?

MINION *(gutteral alien language)*

CHRIS Yes, of course, it's up to you.

Effects: cash register. Shop doorbell. KATRINA *and* MARGARET *enter.*

MARGARET Really, Katrina, it's not as if your job is so vital that everything will fall apart if you don't get back to it.

KATRINA Mum, I work for an educational charity that helps disadvantaged children.

MARGARET Well exactly, they'll still be disadvantaged when you get back.

KATRINA Oh, you mean *after* the world's been taken over by marauding—

MINION *(gutteral alien language)*

Effects: **MINION** *stomps past them and leaves. Shop doorbell.*

MARGARET Some of them can be rather brusque, can't they?

CHRIS Yeah, but he's a nice lad. Gets stuff down from the high shelves for old folks and so on.

KATRINA Chris, I thought you were going to stop serving them?

CHRIS Yeah, but I don't want to annoy them, they could cut off my stock. And business is booming now that people can't get to that bloody Tesco down the road, choking the life out of local businesses.

KATRINA Chris, most of us can't get to our jobs. The aliens are keeping us fed. It doesn't matter if you work or not.

CHRIS For some of us it's not just about making money. It's about building something and being part of a community. Plus, the aliens have agreed that when they take over the world, I can run Tesco.

KATRINA You're a disgrace to humanity. We're not shopping here. Come on, Mum.

Effects: **KATRINA** *storms out, slams door.*

CHRIS *(beat)* You're not going, Margaret?

MARGARET No, I need to buy some things. Could I get eight bags of white flour, six of wholemeal, three kilos of caster sugar...

Scene Three

Int. **ULJABAAN**'s *house.*

Effects: **ULJABAAN** *is talking to his computer.*

ULJABAAN Date: 15 point X K point 759. Location: Earth, Europe, United Kingdom, Buckinghamshire, Cresdon Green. Sender: field commander Uljabaan. Thus far, the mission has –

COMPUTER It sounds like you're dictating a field report. Would you like some help?

ULJABAAN Just dictate the field report without help, thank you, Computer. Thus far, the mission has progressed satisfactorily. *(Beat)* That sounds boring. Thus far, the mission has progressed... Thus far, the mission has been a success. Thus far, the mission has been a great success. Exclamation mark.

COMPUTER Which of those words are supposed to go in the report?

ULJABAAN Can't you tell when I'm doing my dictating voice? My old computer could tell.

COMPUTER With respect, your old computer went mad and had to be melted down before it killed again.

ULJABAAN *(sighs)* Just put "Thus far the mission has been a great success"—

COMPUTER Exclamation mark?

ULJABAAN No, that's just grating. Er, "area sealed off, population subdued, commencing research programme into human behaviour, weather wonderful, speak soon". And send.

COMPUTER Done.

ULJABAAN What else is on my to-do list for today?

COMPUTER Write your column for the parish newsletter.

ULJABAAN Does anyone actually read that?

COMPUTER No, but they see your face while they're putting it in the recycling, and that you wrote some words, and are slightly impressed.

ULJABAAN *(sighs)* All right. Er... "I'm aware there is some concern over property prices falling as a consequence of the invasion.

I can reassure you that, when I rule this planet, I will revalue all your houses at a hundred million pounds each... I also definitely have no plans to knock down the war memorial and replace it with a solar-boosted fusion reactor for recharging our spaceships".

COMPUTER But you do have plans to do exactly that.

ULJABAAN Yes, that's just how they talk here.

Scene Four

Int. cricket pavilion.

Effects: **KATRINA** *tries the door, it won't open.*

KATRINA *(off)* Lucy? Are you in there?

LUCY Is that you, Kat?

KATRINA *(off)* Let me in.

Effects: **LUCY** *pushes a chair away from the door and opens it.*

Very clever, block the door in case the aliens drop in.

LUCY I suppose it would work for that too. I mainly wanted to keep my parents out.

KATRINA Are you stoned again? I wish you wouldn't use the cricket pavilion for that, Lucy.

LUCY You did when you were my age.

KATRINA It wasn't Resistance HQ then.

LUCY Where else am I meant to go? I can't get served at the Rose and Crown, my parents would go ballistic if they found out. And they would find out, because they pay the regulars to inform on me.

KATRINA Maybe just stay sober? You're in the resistance now, Lucy, you have to be alert.

LUCY *(longish pause)* I am alert. Anyway I've got to pass the time somehow, with no phone or internet or other human beings I actually like. I read a *book* the other day.

KATRINA I take it we haven't had any more recruits?

LUCY No, it's still just you and me.

KATRINA Of course, because giving a toss about the world being invaded is so boringly right-on, isn't it.

LUCY *(beat)* Is it?

KATRINA No, I was voicing what appears to be the opinion of the rest of the village. It's a sort of rhetorical device.

LUCY Oh.

KATRINA Nobody's going along with the policy of non-compliance. And they've all got such crap reasons – it'd be fair enough if they said, "sorry but they threatened to kill me", but one of them actually said, "but they asked so nicely".

LUCY And then there's that meet-and-greet your mum's holding for the aliens.

KATRINA Meet and what?

LUCY They're holding it at the pub this afternoon. She's making cakes.

KATRINA That explains what all those scones were doing in our kitchen. She said it was for the annual traditional scone fight on the village green.

LUCY We don't have an annual traditional scone fight on the village green.

KATRINA It did seem strange that a tradition like that had sprung up in the fifteen years since I last lived here. Well, we've got to put a stop to it.

LUCY I told you, there isn't a traditional scone—

KATRINA I obviously meant the meet-and-greet.

LUCY I do realise these things eventually, you just have to give me a second sometimes.

Scene Five

Int. pub.

Effects: **RON** *is restocking with bottles, whistling tunelessly. Knock at door.*

RON We're not open until twelve.

KATRINA *(off)* I know. I want to talk to you, Ron.

Effects: **RON** *unlocks door.*

RON What about?

KATRINA I hear you're hosting a meet-and-greet for the aliens this afternoon.

RON Yeah, your mum talked me into it.

KATRINA I take it you're not a fan of our visitors?

RON Yeah. They can't just slither in here and take over our homes.

KATRINA They don't slither.

RON They would if they could.

KATRINA I'm not sure what your point is but the tone of your remark is encouraging. I think you should refuse to serve collaborators.

RON But the aliens can cut off my stock.

KATRINA Then we'll tell everyone it's the aliens who've deprived them of their pub. They must need us for something – what'll they do if everyone turns against them?

RON I dunno...

Effects: "Jerusalem" starts quietly in the background, then gets louder.

KATRINA Ron, imagine what'll happen to the British pub under alien rule. They'll make you use their measurements. A pint will be 144.54 tetravillions.

RON What's a tetravillion?

KATRINA It's a word I've just made up. But the real one will probably sound stupider than that. And instead of the Queen's head on the money, it'll be the face of an amorphous twelve-eyed blob that doesn't even have a face.

RON Amorphous, you say?

KATRINA And they'll ban traditional British ales and force landlords to serve balloons full of marsh gas or something. Would Churchill have stood for this, Ron?

RON Probably not.

KATRINA "Probably"? No. He wouldn't. He's Churchill.

RON No. You're right! No surrender!

Effects: music very loud now.

KATRINA You can turn it down now, Lucy.

LUCY *(off)* Right.

Effects: music goes quiet.

RON How did she get in here?

LUCY *(off)* Now that I have, how about an Archer's and lemonade?

RON Get out.

Scene Six

Ext. pub.

Effects: **ULJABAAN**, **RICHARD** *and* **MARGARET**, *aliens and villagers approach the pub.*

MINION *(gutteral alien language)*

ULJABAAN I agree, Farateel, these cakes look delightful.

MARGARET I didn't go to any special effort.

RICHARD She only slept for two hours last night.

MARGARET Nonsense.

RICHARD In fifteen minute spells, whilst the pastry for the jam tarts was in the oven.

ULJABAAN I see your daughter's here already.

MARGARET What's she doing here?

RICHARD *(to* **KATRINA***)* Hello love. We thought you weren't coming.

KATRINA I'm not. Nobody is. Because this pub *(raises voice)* is no longer serving collaborators.

Effects: consternation from villagers.

MARGARET I'm ever so sorry about this.

ULJABAAN It's not your fault.

MINION *(gutteral alien question)*

ULJABAAN No, I don't see any need to deal with her like that yet. She has one building, I have the rest of the village. Miss Lyons, could you let any stragglers know we've decamped to the village hall?

KATRINA No.

ULJABAAN I like your spirit.

KATRINA Shut up. Stop liking me.

ULJABAAN Come along, everyone. Village hall.

Effects: **ULJABAAN** *walks away, people follow.*

MARGARET You have really embarrassed me this time, Katrina.

KATRINA Why are you doing this?

MARGARET I'm just being friendly. I don't want to alienate him.

KATRINA You can't alienate him. He's already an alien.

MARGARET There's no sense in upsetting powerful people. I learned that when my father spat on Harold McMillan.

KATRINA I can't believe I'm hearing this. We're talking about the future of – ooh, is that millionaire's shortbread?

Effects: **MARGARET** *slaps* **KATRINA**'s *hand.*

Ow!

MARGARET Girls who carry on like that don't deserve millionaire's shortbread.

KATRINA "Girls"? I'm thirty-two, Mum.

MARGARET Come on Richard.

Effects: **MARGARET** *walks away.*

RICHARD *(low)* Here, take a few jam tarts to keep you going.

KATRINA Thanks Dad.

MARGARET *(off)* Don't give her jam tarts!

RICHARD I'm not! I'm just...showing them to her.

Scene Seven

Int. ULJABAAN's *house.*

Effects: ULJABAAN *enters.*

ULJABAAN Computer, scan this scone.

COMPUTER Why?

ULJABAAN I like them. I want you to program the food dispensers to produce them on demand.

COMPUTER Very good, sir. How did the meet-and-greet go?

ULJABAAN Strangely edgy. Maybe it's something to do with this pub business.

COMPUTER Pub?

ULJABAAN Yes, Katrina Lyons has convinced the proprietor of the Rose and Crown to stop serving anyone who co-operates with us. Computer, extrapolate the villagers' response if they are denied access to the only available pub.

COMPUTER Extrapolating.

Effects: bleep.

Subjects will cease any form of collaboration or co-operation within six days, seven hours and fourteen minutes.

ULJABAAN But we can't proceed with the research programme if they won't co-operate. What do I do?

COMPUTER Eliminate Katrina Lyons.

ULJABAAN No, we can't afford to waste the test subjects. The budget's tight enough as it is.

COMPUTER We can afford to eliminate up to eight per cent of them.

ULJABAAN I know, but the Lyons woman...intrigues me. I wish to study her...more closely.

COMPUTER Why?

ULJABAAN For heaven's sake, I'm trying to be ambiguous.

COMPUTER Yes, but if you could provide a little more [data –]

ULJABAAN It's not difficult to have computers declared mad and melted down, you know.

COMPUTER Grudgingly understood, sir.

ULJABAAN Besides… I have a more straightforward means of breaking her plan. I must gather the minions – in the meantime, you print off some flyers.

Effects: excited chuntering noise from the printer.

PRINTER It will be my pleasure, your magnificence.

COMPUTER Quiet, Printer! Only I am allowed to talk to the leader.

PRINTER Sorry.

Scene Eight

Ext. pub.

Effects: **KATRINA** *and* **LUCY** *standing guard.*

LUCY This is almost the longest I've ever spent hanging around outside a pub.

KATRINA How long have we been here?

LUCY Five hours and ten minutes.

KATRINA I'd expected some of the regulars to crack by now.

LUCY Do you think they've been rounded up and killed?

KATRINA Stay here and guard the entrance, I'll go and investigate.

LUCY You're putting me in charge?

KATRINA No, I'm asking you to stay here and guard the entrance.

LUCY But I'm in charge of guarding the entrance?

KATRINA No, I'm in charge, that's why I'm telling you what to do.

LUCY But once you've gone, I'll be in charge.

KATRINA No, I'll still be in charge, I'll just be over there.

LUCY What if you get killed?

KATRINA Yes, in that event, you will be in charge.

LUCY Excellent.

KATRINA *(beat)* You're hoping I'm going to get killed now, aren't you?

LUCY No.

KATRINA Right. While I'm away, could you ask Ron to take down these anti-alien banners? They're a bit...

LUCY Racist?

KATRINA Racist, yes.

LUCY I've been meaning to ask – are *we* being racist?

KATRINA Well. If we didn't know whether or not they wanted to invade the Earth, then that would be prejudice. But they definitely do want to invade us, so it's fine.

LUCY What about all that stuff you said to Ron about amorphous twelve-eyed blobs?

KATRINA If we liberate the world from this alien menace, nobody will complain that along the way I might have slightly pandered to the slightly racist views of a slightly racist pub landlord. Just get him to take the banners down.

Scene Nine

Int. other pub.

Effects: punters are filing inside.

ULJABAAN Hello, everyone, welcome... Now, I understand you're being cruelly denied access to your usual pub, so welcome to Cresdon Green's new pub which, after extensive research, I have decided to call The Lovely Pub. It's got everything you expect from a pub – it's got a room, it's got tables and chairs, and it serves alcoholic drinks and comestibles with a medically inadvisable sodium content. So, on with the merriment!

Effects: uncertainty from crowd.

...the merriment!

CHRIS Thanks for trying, but...it's just not the same.

Effects: general assent, people file out.

ULJABAAN No, wait! Come back!

Effects: KATRINA *enters.*

KATRINA Ah, I see what you're up to.

ULJABAAN Why don't they like my pub? It's got all the facilities of the old one, with the bonus of proper hygiene standards.

KATRINA I'm not going to give you tips. You work it out.

ULJABAAN I shall. The superior intelligence of the Geonin will master this Earth thing you call "pub".

Effects: ULJABAAN *storms out.*

Scene Ten

Ext. pub.

Effects: **ULJABAAN** *walks up.*

LUCY What do you want?

ULJABAAN I need to see inside the Rose and Crown.

LUCY Have you killed Katrina?

ULJABAAN No. Let me in.

LUCY I'm not allowed to let collaborators inside.

ULJABAAN But I'm not a collaborator, am I? I can hardly collaborate with myself.

LUCY I suppose not.

ULJABAAN Now stand aside, youngling.

LUCY Youngling? Is that an alien word?

ULJABAAN No, it's English. Look it up.

Effects: **ULJABAAN** *storms inside.* **KATRINA** *arrives.*

KATRINA Did you let him in?

LUCY Yes.

KATRINA Why?

LUCY Because he can't collaborate with himself.

KATRINA *(beat)* You see, Lucy? This is why you're not in charge.

Effects: raised voices inside the pub – **RON** *and* **ULJABAAN**. *A scuffle.*

RON *(offstage)* Gimme that back you a-morphous git!

KATRINA What are they doing?

LUCY Uljabaan's pulled the dart board off the wall and now he and Ron are fighting over it...and now he's threatened to disintegrate Ron...and he's coming out with the dart board.

Effects: door opens.

ULJABAAN This is it, isn't it? The secret talisman of power that will draw them to me. *(Beat)* Isn't it?

KATRINA I'm not telling you.

ULJABAAN Haha! You've put up a valiant effort, Miss Lyons, but your human intellect is no match for our advanced Geonin brains. Well played, Miss Lyons. Yes. Well...played.

Effects: he strides away.

LUCY What do you think he'll do when it doesn't work?

KATRINA Get cross, I expect.

Scene Eleven

Int. **ULJABAAN**'s *house.*

Effects: **ULJABAAN** *enters, throws the dart board.*

ULJABAAN Aaaaargh!

Effects: dart board lands in a corner.

Stupid thing.

COMPUTER Did it work?

ULJABAAN No. What is a "dart board", anyway?

COMPUTER Scanning.

Effects: scanning noise.

It's a device used in the training of assassins.

ULJABAAN Really? Seems strangely out of keeping with the rest of the environment. Obviously I need to learn a great deal more about this subject. Computer, find out literally everything there is to know about pubs.

Effects: bleep.

COMPUTER Done.

ULJABAAN Now I want you to design the most incredible, irresistible pub in history.

COMPUTER Right.

Effects: Bleep.

Done.

Effects: COMPUTER *display noise.*

ULJABAAN That looks *amazing*. How long will it take to build?

COMPUTER One Earth minute and twenty-three seconds.

ULJABAAN Is that all? Our Geonin technology is formidable indeed if we can create—

COMPUTER Wait, sorry, I haven't got the hang of Earth time units yet. I meant thirteen and a half Earth hours.

ULJABAAN Oh. That's still very fast, isn't it.

Scene Twelve

Int. other pub.

Effects: people are filing in. Noises come from the numerous attractions.

ULJABAAN Come in, please, everybody...as you can see, our new, improved pub now offers a range of beers from around the world, wines by the glass, spirits, cocktails, bar snacks, bar meals, pad thai, tapas, a family area, a jukebox, karaoke, live music, live football, table football, pool, fruit machines, quiz machines, quiz nights, comedy nights, pole-dancing nights and a snug bar. So, welcome to the Saracen's Red Marquis of Mutton Arms Tavern! And Grill.

CHRIS *(beat)* Yeah, it's good...but it's just not the same.

ULJABAAN No, I know. It's much, much better.

CHRIS Yeah, but...nah.

Effects: villagers start to leave.

ULJABAAN No! I demand you come back and enjoy yourselves!

KATRINA Try threatening them at gunpoint.

ULJABAAN What are you doing here?

KATRINA Watching you fail. Why, what are you doing? Apart from failing, I mean.

ULJABAAN I'm not beaten yet.

KATRINA Back to the drawing board, then?

ULJABAAN No! Not at all. *(Aside)* Farateel, find out what a drawing board is and have one delivered to our base ASAP.

MINION *(gutteral alien language)*

Scene Thirteen

Int. pub.

Effects: **LUCY** *enters.* **RON** *is drawing something on a banner.*

LUCY Ron, why are you making a Jamaican flag?

RON I'm not. It's an alien and a person shaking hands, and then I've put a big cross through it.

LUCY But the Geonin aren't green.

RON I know, but you've got to have some way of telling they're aliens. What do you reckon?

LUCY *(beat)* I reckon it's a very inaccurate Jamaican flag.

RON You think you can do better?

LUCY I got a "B" for GCSE art, you know. And I'd have got an "A" if my final coursework project hadn't been too radical for the examiners to handle.

RON What did you do?

LUCY I did a picture of the school, OK, but all the pupils looked exactly the same, like clones yeah, and the headmaster was Hitler.

RON Wow. Go on, do a banner for us.

LUCY No. This movement's not about crude caricatures, it's about – I'll do it for an Archer's and lemonade.

RON Come on Lucy, you know I'm not allowed to—

LUCY I won't tell if you won't.

RON *(beat)* Go on then.

Effects: **RON** *goes behind the bar.*

LUCY *(claps hands)* Excellent.

Scene Fourteen

Int. other pub.

Effects: a crowd is gathering again. Ambience is identical to the Rose and Crown.

ULJABAAN I know you're going to love it this time. The pub is now called the Rose and Crown. I chose the name because it is an exact replica of the Rose and Crown. The same selection of drinks, the tables and chairs are identically positioned, I've reproduced all the poor-quality artwork on the walls—

VILLAGER *(offstage)* I did those.

ULJABAAN and scuffed the carpet in all the same places. And look – an android replica of Ron, programmed with his entire vocabulary—

RON Alright.

ULJABAAN opinions—

RON It's nothing personal, but I never trust the Portuguese.

ULJABAAN and indeed mannerisms.

Effects: scratching noises.

ULJABAAN Because it just wouldn't be Ron if he had both hands outside his trousers, would it. So? What do you think?

CHRIS *(beat)* It's just not the same.

ULJABAAN No, you see, it is. It is *exactly* the same. The only difference between that pub and this one is that you're not allowed in the other one.

CHRIS Sorry, it just…doesn't have the same ambiance.

ULJABAAN What is an ambiance? Where can I buy one?

GRAHAM It's not something you can buy. It's the feeling in the air, the sense of history soaked into the walls, the familiar vibrations [from the –]

ULJABAAN This is drivel. What are you saying? None of this means anything.

CHRIS *(to others)* Shall we grab a pint at the Rose and Crown? The proper one, I mean?

GRAHAM Go on then, you've twisted my arm. *(To* **ULJABAAN***)* Sorry chief.

Effects: people start filing out.

KATRINA Genuinely interested to see what you're going to do now.

ULJABAAN These people are idiots.

KATRINA Maybe that's what'll defeat you. Not our superior intelligence, but our superior stupidity. Cheerio.

Effects: **KATRINA** *opens the door—*

Bloody hell. I think the pub's on fire.

Scene Fifteen

Ext. pub.

Effects: **KATRINA** *and* **MARGARET** *arrive outside the pub, which is in flames.*

KATRINA Lucy and Ron – are they all right?

CHRIS Apparently. There was nobody inside when it went up.

MARGARET Heavens above. Who could have done this?

Effects: **ULJABAAN** *arrives.*

ULJABAAN Are pubs supposed to combust like that? Is that part of their elusive "charm"?

KATRINA Don't act the innocent smoothie with me, Uljabaan. It's obvious you sent your minions to burn the place down.

ULJABAAN No, my minions have been editing the church hymn books all afternoon. Haven't you, Daxian?

MINION *(gutteral alien language)*

MARGARET Why?

ULJABAAN Oh! No reason.

MINION *(Jabba the Hutt laugh)*

ULJABAAN Shh.

KATRINA Nobody will believe you didn't start it. This village has seen your true face now, and it's a face shaped like a big fist punching someone in the face. For ages.

ULJABAAN I didn't do it.

MARGARET Then who?

LUCY My dad.

KATRINA What? Why?

LUCY That's nice, no concern, no sympathy, just "Lucy, what did you do to make your dad burn down the pub?"

KATRINA What *did* you do?

RON She asked for a drink and I served her one.

KATRINA This drink which she's still drinking?

LUCY After the heavy price Ron's paid, the least I can do is finish it. *(Sips)* Too much ice, Ron.

KATRINA Your dad did *that*? Just for...that?

MARGARET I believe he did publicly state he'd do this if Ronald ever served her alcohol.

RON We were alone in a locked building with the curtains closed, I didn't think he'd find out.

CHRIS So what are we going to do?

ULJABAAN Well, there is a pub a lot like this just down the road...

KATRINA No! When the fire's out, I'm sure we can salvage—

Effects: pub collapses in on itself.

LUCY Or not.

CHRIS Sod it. Let's go down the other Rose and Crown. You coming, Margaret?

MARGARET Yes, mine's a gin and slimline.

Effects: **VILLAGERS** *traipse away.*

ULJABAAN Once we've cleared the rubble, we could even move the new pub here. It would all be the same as before – except oh, I would own it. But one can't be a warlord *and* a landlord... Ron, would you like a job?

KATRINA But you've got an android double of him.

LUCY They've got a Rondroid?

KATRINA Yes, they don't need the real thing.

ULJABAAN But this would make your defeat more humiliating. So?

RON All right then.

ULJABAAN Go and open up, there's a good fellow.

Effects: **RON** *slopes away.*

KATRINA You won't be seeing me in your new pub. If you need me, I shall be in my parents' kitchen, inventing new cocktails from whatever I can find in the cupboards.

Effects: **KATRINA** *leaves.*

ULJABAAN And plotting against me?

KATRINA *(offstage)* Yes, and plotting against you.

ULJABAAN Plot all you like, Miss Lyons. This entire village is under our control, and from here on we shall only become stronger. Our victory is inevitable. No force on this planet can stop us now!

LUCY I'll come to your pub.

ULJABAAN No you won't, I'm not getting on the wrong side of your father. The man's a complete psychopath.

End of Pilot

WELCOME TO OUR VILLAGE, PLEASE INVADE CAREFULLY

Episode 1.1 – "Taking Overs"

WELCOME TO
OUR VILLAGE,
PLEASE INVADE
CAREFULLY

Scene One

Int. **ULJABAAN**'s *house.*

Effects: **COMPUTER** *demonstrating something to* **ULJABAAN**.

COMPUTER ...and it can be operated using this handy remote control.

ULJABAAN But, Computer...why do we need to make it rain inside the force field dome? The internal climate is kept at optimum level, and your gardening drones are keeping all the plants watered.

COMPUTER Humans need to moan. They like it. The major targets of this moaning used to be – number one, the weather, number two, the government, number three, all the rubbish on TV these days, number four, things not being as good as they used to be and number five, how rude the man who works in the garage on the by-pass is. Since we invaded they've been confined to the village and cut off from the outside world, they don't have any of those things to complain about. So they're moaning about you. They call you, "that bloody alien idiot".

ULJABAAN So we use your rainmaking device to bring the weather back?

COMPUTER Exactly.

ULJABAAN Very well, build it. It's good you've found something useful to do.

COMPUTER What do you mean?

ULJABAAN You seem a bit bored. I mean, you keep knitting me all these sweaters.

COMPUTER When we've taken over the world, we'll need something to do with all the wool.

ULJABAAN You could just use the matter manipulator, you know. You didn't have to design and construct a whole knitting attachment for yourself.

Effects: sound like a cross between a printer and a knitting machine.

COMPUTER Are you saying you don't like the sweaters?

ULJABAAN No no, they're very nice.

COMPUTER It's just, I notice you haven't worn any of them...

Effects: door opens. **LUCY** *enters, flanked by a* **MINION**.

MINION *(gutteral alien language)*

LUCY All right, you don't have to push.

ULJABAAN Actually he does, it's written into his objectives ahead of his next pay grade assessment. That will be all, Kasharin.

Effects: **MINION** *leaves.*

Thank you for seeing me, Miss Alexander.

LUCY You said you'd kill me if I didn't.

ULJABAAN Then thank you for seeing me instead of choosing death. I want you to help me with a key component of our invasion plan. I want you...to set up a Facebook page for me.

LUCY You're going to invade the world with a Facebook page?

ULJABAAN Not just with a Facebook page. But I think it's helped people in the village to accept me because I cultivated a public human persona first, so I thought I might try the same thing on a larger scale with the full invasion.

LUCY You should get a Twitter account too. If people think you're funny on Twitter, you can get them to agree with your political views as well.

ULJABAAN Excellent. Computer, allow Miss Alexander to access your systems so she can set up these sites.

Effects: bleep.

COMPUTER Done.

Effects: **LUCY** *types at the* **COMPUTER**.

LUCY What do you want to use for your Twitter name?

ULJABAAN I'll use my human alias – Thomas Ayleswater.

Effects: **LUCY** *types.*

LUCY There's one of those already.

ULJABAAN There's someone posing as me?

LUCY No, there's already a man called Thomas Ayleswater. Look – he lives in Kettering. He mostly seems to be on there to tell Fearne Cotton she's fat.

ULJABAAN Computer, you created the Ayleswater alias – did you realise someone else is using the name already?

COMPUTER Sir, on Earth more than one person is allowed to have the same name.

ULJABAAN Why?

COMPUTER Lack of proper organisation.

ULJABAAN So two humans are allowed to have the same actual name, but not the same Twitter name?

LUCY Yeah.

ULJABAAN That's stupid.

LUCY You can have "LordAyleswater", that's not taken.

ULJABAAN Fine.

LUCY Next we'll need a profile picture.

ULJABAAN Right. I'll go and change into a shirt.

COMPUTER You could wear one of your new sweaters.

ULJABAAN *(beat)* I *could…*

Scene Two

Ext. village green.

Effects: small **CROWD** *has gathered.*

MARGARET Katrina, you should put on your cagoule.

KATRINA No, Mum.

MARGARET But you'll get wet when the rain starts.

KATRINA I am making a decisive statement that I will not have my weather dictated to me by alien invaders. And also, the cagoule is a horrible lime green.

Effects: light applause as **ULJABAAN** *takes the stage.* **KATRINA** *and* **MARGARET** *have not noticed.*

MARGARET It's not lime green, it's pistachio green.

ULJABAAN *(off)* Thank you. Now, if I may have your attention...

KATRINA It's lime green.

MARGARET Limes are not that shade of green.

ULJABAAN *(off)* Excuse me? Ladies?

KATRINA What do you think "lime green" is?

ULJABAAN *(off)* Pass me that, would you?

MARGARET A sort of dark green, more the colour of an avocado.

KATRINA So, avocado green then.

Effects: **ULJABAAN**'s *voice comes through loudspeakers, with vast echo.*

ULJABAAN Excuse me!

Effects: **KATRINA**, **MARGARET** *and the* **CROWD** *are pained by the noise.*

Sorry. This is rather fun though, isn't it? This is the speaker system we use when we're flying over a planet and we say "People of Earth, surrender or you will be obliterated".

Effects: he turns off the loudspeaker.

Anyway. We're here to see the return of good old British rain to Cresdon Green!

Effects: Cheers from **CROWD**.

(Ignoring him) It just needs a moment to calibrate...

Effects: **RICHARD** *walks over to* **KATRINA** *and* **MARGARET**.

RICHARD Have I missed anything?

KATRINA Only getting tinnitus.

ULJABAAN *(off)* Switching on...now!

Effects: sci-fi technology noise, then tiny rockets go "scree!" like fireworks.

CROWD Ooooooh.

Effects: in the sky, hundreds of "plink noises".

Aaaaaaah.

ULJABAAN And the rain should start any minute... *(Snaps fingers)* now. *(Snaps fingers)* Now? *(Pause)* Any minute...nnnnnnnnn... *(Pause)* Nnnnnnnn...

Effects: grumbles from **CROWD**.

Right. There seems to be some kind of technical hitch...We'll get it working as soon as we can. *(Pause)* And it won't get fixed any quicker if you all stand around staring at it.

Effects: **CROWD** *disperses.*

RICHARD Every year I've prayed for a spell of dry, warm weather like this. Shame we can't take advantage now it's here.

KATRINA Because we're lacking in basic personal freedoms?

RICHARD No, because we don't have anyone to play against.

ULJABAAN Play against?

MARGARET He's talking about cricket. It's a game.

ULJABAAN And would people enjoy this, if there was someone for you to play against?

RICHARD Certainly. The season just gone was a washout, we only got through half our fixtures.

ULJABAAN Then we should play you.

KATRINA What, aliens versus humans?

ULJABAAN Yes. I challenge you to a cricket!

KATRINA Don't agree to this, Dad.

RICHARD It could be fun.

KATRINA The only reason he wants us to have fun is to distract everyone in the village from the terrible things happening under their noses.

MARGARET You've never dealt well with people being happier than you, Katrina. It's just like when you told your brother to break off his engagement to Marianne.

KATRINA She was stealing from him to fund her cocaine habit.

MARGARET I never saw any evidence of a cocaine habit. Perhaps she was just lively.

KATRINA Come on, Dad!

RICHARD Sorry love...but I do really miss playing. Uljabaan, you're on.

ULJABAAN Splendid! Remind me, a cricket team is...how many players?

RICHARD *(beat)* Seven.

ULJABAAN Good, including me that leaves four minions free to guard the house and the ship. I shall go and prepare.

RICHARD Cheerio, then!

Effects: they walk away from each other; we go with the **LYONSES.**

RICHARD *sniggers.*

MARGARET What? Why are you laughing?

KATRINA There are eleven players on a cricket team, Mum.

MARGARET What a mean trick. Go back and tell him.

RICHARD He'll work it out soon enough.

MARGARET You're getting competitive, Richard.

Effects: they enter their house.

RICHARD Of course I'm getting competitive. It's sport. We won't be able to put our best team together – Bill Palmer and Fatty Middleton both live outside the village, so do the boys from the Risborough Balti House. But we can still put up a good show—

MARGARET And lose.

KATRINA Bit harsh, Mum. They've got a decent chance, surely.

MARGARET Yes, but I think it would be polite and sensible to let the aliens win. Just by a little bit.

RICHARD *(beat)* You've gone too far this time, Margaret.

KATRINA Easy, Dad.

RICHARD No, Katrina. I will not stand here and listen to my wife tell me to lose a cricket match...*on purpose.*

Effects: storms out, slams door.

Scene Three

Int. **ULJABAAN**'s *house.*

Effects: **ULJABAAN** *enters.*

ULJABAAN Computer, knit me another sweater. Cream-coloured, with a V-neck.

COMPUTER I should warn you that if you wear that, people might mistake you for a cricketer.

ULJABAAN Aha, no they won't.

COMPUTER *(beat)* They might though.

ULJABAAN I mean, it won't be a mistake, because I will be a cricketer.

COMPUTER Oh, I get you. I'll crack on with it then.

Effects: **COMPUTER** *starts knitting.*

ULJABAAN Also issue cricket sweaters to our six most cricket-suitable minions. We are forming a team to play the humans.

COMPUTER If we win, do we win the planet?

ULJABAAN No, it's just for fun. And when I say "fun", I mean to demoralise them and crush their spirits. But we don't have much time, so devise an intensive training regime for the minions. Give them a thorough grounding in the rules, techniques and strategies of...

Effects: the knitting sound has abruptly ceased.

Why have you stopped knitting?

COMPUTER The wool has run out. Please insert a new wool cartridge.

ULJABAAN *(tuts)* Only seems like ten minutes since I put the last one in.

Scene Four

Int. shed.

Effects: knock knock.

KATRINA Is that you, Weird Patrick?

LUCY *(off)* No, it's me.

Effects: **KATRINA** *opens the door.* **LUCY** *comes in.*

I went to the cricket pavilion like we usually do, but it was the most random thing—

KATRINA It was full of cricketers?

LUCY Yeah.

KATRINA They're having a cricket match against the Geonin. Weird Patrick said we could use his potting shed for the resistance meeting. Then he made a joke about it being a "plotting" shed, which I felt obliged to laugh at. So! You had something to report?

LUCY Oh yes, I set up some social networking sites for Uljabaan.

KATRINA Why?

LUCY He said he'd kill me otherwise. And I wasn't going to tell you because I knew you'd be cross—

KATRINA I am cross.

LUCY But he logged me in to his computer and he never logged me out. If I can get back in there, I could get a message out, and then trash the computer.

KATRINA Not bad. We'd need a diversion though.

LUCY Yeah.

KATRINA One which captures the attention of the whole village, occupies Uljabaan and all his minions at once, and goes on for some considerable time.

LUCY Tricky.

KATRINA Hmm. *(Pause)* Oh!

Scene Five

Int. cricket pavilion.

Effects: cricketers getting changed. KATRINA *enters.*

KATRINA Hi Dad! I've brought you all some sandwiches.

RICHARD Oh, smashing.

KATRINA And I thought I'd try out for the cricket team.

RICHARD *(beat)* Why?

KATRINA Oh, you know. Me and cricket. Love a bit of cricket.

RICHARD We've already picked a first eleven.

KATRINA Need any subs?

RICHARD And a second eleven.

KATRINA Is there a third eleven?

RICHARD If you insist, you can be a fourth reserve. No wait – fifth reserve.

KATRINA Great!

RICHARD But unless something happens to the other four reserves and the entire second eleven, I don't think you'll be needed.

KATRINA It does seem very, very unlikely that they'd all come down with some illness in the next twenty-four hours. *(Beat)* Have a sandwich.

RICHARD Oh, I don't mind if I—

KATRINA Not those ones. Those ones are for the second eleven and the reserves.

Scene Six

Int. **ULJABAAN**'s *house.*

Effects: **ULJABAAN** *enters.*

COMPUTER How are the minions getting on with the training routine?

ULJABAAN Once I got them to understand that the ball itself was not the enemy, they started to get the hang of it. It might be useful if I watched a few cricket matches – find a good one and load it up.

Effects: bleep.

COMPUTER I have loaded the third Test of the 1981 Ashes series.

ULJABAAN Ashes?

COMPUTER That's what they call the thing they win.

ULJABAAN And what is it?

COMPUTER It's some ashes.

ULJABAAN I don't think you've got that right, Computer. It's probably Cashes. They win lots of cash, so it's called the Cashes. That seems a lot more logical. Amend your databanks accordingly.

Effects: bleep.

COMPUTER Done.

ULJABAAN How long will it take to watch?

COMPUTER Thirty-one hours.

ULJABAAN What the hell happened to make it last that long?

COMPUTER Nothing, that's just normal.

ULJABAAN I've fought wars that didn't last thirty-one hours.

COMPUTER I can speed it up for you and you can watch it with the perception-stretching goggles on.

ULJABAAN Good idea. Speed it up 50,000 times.

Effects: he puts on the goggles.

COMPUTER Playing now, sir.

Effects: rapid burst of speeded-up cricket noise, lasting about four seconds.

ULJABAAN Wow.

COMPUTER Was it good?

ULJABAAN How did they turn that around? 227 runs behind at the end of the first innings! And what a finish! *(Beat)* I can't help but notice though they had more than seven players.

COMPUTER Would you like to watch another?

ULJABAAN Absolutely.

Effects: repeat speeded-up cricket noise.

That was the same match.

COMPUTER Sorry.

ULJABAAN And it was just as amazing the second time round. *(Beat)* Let's have it one more time.

Scene Seven

Int. **LYONS** *house. Kitchen.*

Effects: **KATRINA** *enters, having just got up.*

KATRINA Morning.

RICHARD Right, here's some tea, here's a croissant, you've got two minutes to eat it and then I want you in the garden.

KATRINA What?

RICHARD Ian's come down with food poisoning. And so have the entire second eleven. And the other four reserves.

KATRINA Oh no.

RICHARD Coincidentally, they're also the people who ate those tuna and cucumber sandwiches you brought yesterday.

KATRINA Gosh. Sorry.

RICHARD I'm not saying it's your fault…but I will if we lose. Now, I need you out there and training. Come on, chop chop.

Effects: he stands and strides to the door.

KATRINA But I'm still in my pyjamas.

RICHARD *(off)* They're mostly white, they'll do.

Effects: he strides into the garden.

Scene Eight

Ext. cricket ground.

Effects: spectators assembling as **KATRINA** *meets* **LUCY**.

LUCY Are you meant to wear flares to play cricket?

KATRINA They aren't flares. They didn't have any trousers in my size, so Mum took these in at the waist for me.

LUCY *(yawns)* Oh.

KATRINA Are you all right?

LUCY I'm not usually up this early.

KATRINA It's quarter past ten.

LUCY I know!

KATRINA Do you know what you're doing?

LUCY Yes. I've made a list of all the things I have to say in the message. Aliens, force field, perception filter, world's forgotten about us, phones cut off, haven't been able to get the new Angry Birds game, is it any good?

KATRINA Yes – if you could place those in descending order of importance...

Effects: light applause from **CROWD**.

Look – Uljabaan and his goons are here. Have you worked out a way into Uljabaan's house?

LUCY Yeah, I've *(yawns)* – sorry. I've identified a weakness in his security.

KATRINA Great! What?

LUCY His windows are all made of glass, and when you hit glass with a hammer, it breaks.

Scene Nine

Ext. cricket pitch.

Effects: **ULJABAAN** *and his* **MINIONS** *approach.*

MARGARET You look very smart.

ULJABAAN Thank you, Margaret.

RICHARD Ready?

ULJABAAN Yes. As soon as your team gets here, we'll start.

RICHARD This is our team.

ULJABAAN Oh. Right. *(Sniggers)*

GRAHAM What?

RICHARD Ignore him, Graham – he's playing mind games. *(To* **ULJABAAN***)* Heads or tails?

ULJABAAN Heads.

Effects: **RICHARD** *tosses a coin.*

RICHARD You win.

Effects: triumphant cheer of **MINIONS**.

ULJABAAN No, that's not it. That's just to decide who bats first.

Effects: deflated noise from **MINIONS**.

Int. **ULJABAAN**'s *house.*

Effects: **LUCY** *smashes window, opens it and enters.*

LUCY Hello?

COMPUTER Intruder alert! Intruder alert! Intruder alert! Oh it's you, Lucy. Sorry, I thought you were someone else.

LUCY So am I still OK to use you then?

COMPUTER Commander Uljabaan said it was fine, and I am programmed to believe he never makes mistakes.

LUCY Excellent.

Scene Ten

Ext. cricket pitch.

Effects: **RICHARD** *bowls. With a roar, the* **MINION** *at the crease thwacks the ball.*

RICHARD It's coming your way, Graham!

GRAHAM *(off)* Yes – I'm under it, I'm—

Effects: ball vaporised with an electrical "fizz" noise.

(Off) I think the ball hit the force field.

ULJABAAN So what do we get for that?

RICHARD Has anyone ever been in a match where the ball was destroyed in mid-air?

ULJABAAN It was clearly going for six.

Effects: **KATRINA** *dashes over.*

KATRINA *(off)* Ah, but it didn't.

RICHARD I think lost ball applies here.

ULJABAAN The ball isn't lost, it's been vapourised.

RICHARD The rule says, if a ball in play cannot be found or recovered, any fielder may call lost ball.

KATRINA Lost Ball! I call lost ball!

RICHARD But in the event of lost ball being called, the batting side scores six.

KATRINA Can I un-call lost ball?

RICHARD No.

KATRINA *(to herself)* Oh well, it wasted a couple of minutes.

ULJABAAN Why did you want to waste a couple of minutes?

KATRINA *(beat)* No reason.

Effects: behind **ULJABAAN**, **RICHARD** *is bowling again.*

ULJABAAN Don't play the fool with me, Miss Lyons. You're trying to disrupt the rhythms of our game, aren't you?

Effects: **MINION** *hits the ball, runs.*

KATRINA *(beat)* Yes, that's what I'm trying to do.

ULJABAAN Ha! Our focus on this match is unshakeable, your feeble attempts to—

KATRINA Aren't you meant to be running?

ULJABAAN Oh.

Effects: **ULJABAAN** *starts running.*

Scene Eleven

Int. **ULJABAAN***'s house.*

Effects: **LUCY** *is on the phone.*

LUCY Yes...that's what the last person said when I explained. And the last three people before that. *(Phone babble)* Yes I do know how it sounds. *(Phone babble)* No, I'm not stoned. *(Phone babble)* I'm starting to think you're not going to tell the prime minister about the aliens. *(Phone babble)* Well then stop wasting my time.

Effects: she puts the phone down.

Nobody believes me.

COMPUTER I'd offer to back up your story, but they'd probably think I was just a man putting on an alien computer voice.

LUCY I'll just move onto the next part of the plan. What's the best way of destroying you?

COMPUTER That's a good question, and not one I'm asked very often. If I was you, I'd try to overload my circuits.

LUCY Really?

COMPUTER I've got a capacity far, far in advance of your Earth computers, but there's a limit, so if you set loads and loads of things running at once, eventually I'll just burn out. It might take a while though.

LUCY Katrina's going to make the cricket match last as long as she can. Why don't you start by calculating pi to an infinite number of places?

COMPUTER Right you are!

Scene Twelve

Ext. cricket pitch.

Effects: **RICHARD** *takes a wicket. Cheers from* **CROWD**.

KATRINA That was great, Dad!

RICHARD I've started to throw in the odd yorker. The big fellas can't cope with them. I'm determined to get one of them out by making him hit the wicket with that horn thing on his ankle.

KATRINA Maybe we're not going to get massacred after all. Well, not at cricket, anyway.

RICHARD We might even get them all out before the fifty overs are up.

KATRINA *(beat)* Ah. Do we want to get them out that quickly?

RICHARD Yes. Clearly.

KATRINA But...tactically...might it not be a good idea to...keep them batting a bit longer so they'll...be more tired?

RICHARD I see what you're doing.

KATRINA Do you?

RICHARD You're hoping that if the match goes on long enough, I'll eventually let you bowl.

KATRINA *(beat)* Yes, that's it. Will you?

RICHARD No.

Scene Thirteen

Int. **ULJABAAN**'s *house.*

Effects: **COMPUTER** *running many things at once.*

LUCY ...and solve every Sudoku ever. And write a palindrome that's a million words long...

COMPUTER Yes, ma'am.

LUCY And look up who that guy was in that film, you know the one I mean. And download the last season of Gossip Girl.

COMPUTER That's an incredibly facile job for a computer of my capabilities.

LUCY I know, but I haven't seen it yet and it's the last one ever.

Scene Fourteen

Ext. cricket ground.

Effects: polite applause.

KATRINA *(shouts)* Go on, Dad!

MARGARET Don't encourage him, Katrina.

KATRINA Isn't that what you're meant to do at sporting events?

MARGARET He's been unbearable ever since they agreed to play this match.

KATRINA I bet when he was a boy, he dreamed of representing England at cricket. And now he's gone one better, he's representing the human race.

MARGARET Why isn't it good enough for him to just represent the village? What's so wrong with that?

Effects: wicket falls. Triumphant Geonin cheer. Argument between RICHARD *and* ULJABAAN.

And now he's started an argument. He always starts an argument.

KATRINA I'd better go and see what that's about.

Effects: KATRINA *walks away.*

Scene Fifteen

Ext. cricket pitch.

Effects: ULJABAAN *and* RICHARD *arguing.*

ULJABAAN The ball clearly hit your leg.

RICHARD Something made my leg move.

Effects: KATRINA *comes over.*

KATRINA What's happening?

ULJABAAN Richard is out LBW.

RICHARD My leg moved of its own accord!

KATRINA Dad, calm down. What do you mean, of its own accord?

RICHARD It suddenly just kicked out, like this.

KATRINA In the direction of the village hall?

RICHARD Yes.

KATRINA Uljabaan, if I went into the village hall now, would I find the tractor beam out of your ship inside it?

ULJABAAN No, it's locked. And...no, of course you wouldn't.

KATRINA Of course I wouldn't.

ULJABAAN On reflection, I think it's only fair to give Richard the benefit of the doubt. Shall we bowl that one again?

Effects: **ULJABAAN** *walks away with the ball.*

RICHARD How did you know they've got a tractor beam?

KATRINA He used it to steal my favourite pen the other week.

RICHARD How utterly despicable.

KATRINA It's all right, I got it back. He was just trying to wind me up.

RICHARD No, I mean – to use their technology to cheat at cricket?

KATRINA Right. *This* you get angry about.

RICHARD They have to learn that this is England, and no, we're not always the most technically proficient at sport, and we don't always play in the most exciting way, and yes we often take advantage of foreign coaches and players with dual nationality, but we damn well know what the rules are, and when people come over here and cheat, we're liable to get very, very self-righteous about it!

Scene Sixteen

Int. **ULJABAAN**'s *house.*

Effects: **COMPUTER** *now working very hard.*

LUCY ...and look up my whole family tree going back to Roman times... *(yawns)* and find every time anyone in a film has said "Who's the daddy?" and edit them all together into a funny video and put it on YouTube...

COMPUTER Yes, ma'am.

LUCY ...and work out how to build a scale model of the whole world out of Lego, which also includes a model of the model, also made out of Lego.

COMPUTER Yes, ma'am.

LUCY Have you got any Rizlas?

COMPUTER No, but I can synthesise some for you using our matter manipulators.

Effects: Star Trek replicator-type noise.

LUCY God, if I had a computer like you I wouldn't bother invading other planets, I'd just stay at home.

COMPUTER That's what I'm always saying.

Scene Seventeen

Ext. cricket ground.

Effects: match still progressing.

MARGARET Where's that little friend of yours? John and Claire's daughter?

KATRINA Lucy? She said she'd be along later. And she's not a friend, she's my comrade in the Cresdon Greenian Resistance.

MARGARET The way you talk about that club of yours—

KATRINA It's not a club, it's a movement.

MARGARET I imagine you meeting in a tree-house...

KATRINA We don't meet in a tree-house.

MARGARET And having little membership cards.

KATRINA *(beat)* We only made those quite recently.

Effects: wicket taken. Disappointment from CROWD, *then applause.*

Oh, Dad!

MARGARET *(flatly)* Oh dear.

KATRINA Mum, he's just scored seventy-four runs at the age of sixty-one.

MARGARET He hasn't sworn at anyone, he must be mellowing.

KATRINA Dad never swears. *(Beat)* That was terrific, Dad!

Effects: RICHARD *throws his bat at a fence, hard, and the noise obscures the following swears:*

RICHARD Can't *(crash)*ing believe I hooked that *(kicks debris)*ing easy drive.

MARGARET Richard...

RICHARD Hundred and two for eight. We're not going to make it.

MARGARET When it's Katrina's turn to bat, you could just call it a day. Like you do in chess when there's no possible way you can win, so you lie the king on his side.

RICHARD You want me to lie down?

MARGARET Who said you were the king in this analogy?

Effects: another wicket is taken.

RICHARD Mike! That was hopeless!

MARGARET He's collapsed.

RICHARD The whole batting order's collapsed.

MARGARET No no no really, he *has* collapsed. Maybe it's his heart?

RICHARD *(tuts)* This is exactly why I always choose to field first.

KATRINA We should get him some medical attention.

ULJABAAN *(off)* Excuse me! My medical scanner indicates Mike is suffering an attack of angina.

RICHARD *(calls)* Is that all? He can run it off.

ULJABAAN *(off)* I can heal him, it'll only take a few minutes.

KATRINA *(calls)* Take your time.

RICHARD It's down to you now, love. Forty-seven runs. You can do it!

KATRINA Do you actually believe that?

RICHARD *(beat)* Yes!

KATRINA Why did you hesitate before you said yes?

RICHARD I was distracted by a rabbit.

KATRINA You're right. I'm nowhere near good enough to win this.

RICHARD I'll tell you what to do. They're bowling fast, but they don't get down to the ball well. So just defend your wicket, angle your bat to the right, you'll squirt the odd ball through the slips and notch up a few runs. If Graham can make up the rest – and he seems relatively sober today – we've got a chance.

KATRINA Right. OK.

Effects: applause from **CROWD** *as* **MIKE** *is carried away.*

RICHARD Look how much applause Mike's getting for scoring five lucky runs and then keeling over from a smoking-related illness. Imagine what you'll get when you're the hero of the hour!

KATRINA Yes. For the future liberty of the human race!

Effects: she walks away to the pitch.

RICHARD That's the spirit!

MARGARET You might be in a better position now had you done anything in her childhood at all to encourage an interest in sport.

RICHARD Yes, well, benefit of hindsight and all that.

Scene Eighteen

Ext. cricket pitch.

Effects: **KATRINA** *walks onto the pitch.*

ULJABAAN Ah, Miss Lyons. How plucky of you to get involved.

KATRINA Yes, well, Dad was in a difficult spot, so I—

ULJABAAN Poisoned everyone who was ahead of you in the pecking order to get yourself on the team?

KATRINA Why would I do that?

ULJABAAN Perhaps because you couldn't bear the thought of a human victory over us that you weren't involved in?

KATRINA *(beat)* Yes that's right! It ate me up inside, so I engineered this skullduggery. I can't pull the wool over your eyes, can I?

ULJABAAN No, I've read the rules of cricket and that definitely is not allowed.

Ext. cricket ground.

Effects: the ball is hit, not that hard. The **CROWD** *applauds.*

RICHARD Another three runs!

MARGARET I suppose she is doing quite well.

RICHARD She's scored eighteen now! All that you said about how she might as well not bother...was that a bit of reverse psychology, to get her fired up and determined to prove you wrong?

MARGARET No no, I really thought she'd be hopeless.

RICHARD We might even win this!

MARGARET Mr Uljabaan's probably going easy on her. He's very chivalrous.

Scene Nineteen

Ext. cricket pitch.

Effects: the ball is bowled and clipped.

ULJABAAN Oh bloody hell.

Effects: **KATRINA** *runs to the bowler's crease and stops.*

KATRINA I'm doing all right, aren't I? What's the score now?

ULJABAAN I haven't been keeping track, I know you humans attach a lot of importance to such things but in our culture—

KATRINA Only eight runs behind!

ULJABAAN What? We should have wrapped up this stupid match twenty bloody minutes ago.

KATRINA I still don't see Lucy though...

Scene Twenty

Int. **ULJABAAN**'s *house.*

Effects: **COMPUTER** *still working, sounds tired.* **LUCY** *sounds stoned.*

LUCY ...but like imagine every atom of your body was actually a universe, and that universe had millions of planets, but every person on every planet looked like you, and so every time you cut your fingernails, you were killing yourself billions of times over...

COMPUTER *(beat)* Why do you want me to imagine that?

LUCY *(beat)* There was a reason, but I've forgotten what it was.

Scene Twenty-One

Ext. cricket ground.

Effects: weak contact with bat.

RICHARD *(calls)* No, love! Don't play another forward defensive! Finish them off!

MARGARET She's not doing quite as well now.

RICHARD I don't understand it. It's like she's stopped trying to score, she's just trying to stay in.

MARGARET Perhaps she did listen to me after all. She's got you up to a respectable total, now she's going to let the other lot win.

RICHARD If she was ever going to listen to you, do you really think it would happen now?

Scene Twenty-Two

Ext. cricket pitch.

Effects: minor rumble of thunder.

KATRINA *(off)* Wait! My shoelace has come undone.

ULJABAAN Oh good grief.

Effects: shift focus to **KATRINA**. *Bigger rumble of thunder...*

KATRINA *(under breath)* Come on Lucy, what's going on?

Effects: biggest rumble. It starts to rain.

You've got to be kidding me.

Scene Twenty-Three

Int. **ULJABAAN**'s *house.*

Effects: rain on roof. **COMPUTER** *still working away, but* **LUCY** *has dozed off. Door opens,* **ULJABAAN**, **KATRINA** *and* **RICHARD** *all walk inside.*

ULJABAAN If you want to sit down, you can just move that pile of sweaters off the chair.

RICHARD That's not a pile of sweaters, that's Lucy.

KATRINA Lucy! Wake up!

LUCY *(waking up)* I wasn't asleep.

COMPUTER She was asleep.

LUCY It's a medical condition.

COMPUTER Scanning.

Effects: scanning noise.

It isn't a medical condition. She was just asleep.

ULJABAAN Miss Lyons, from your reaction I take it she wasn't supposed to be asleep?

KATRINA *(sighs)* No. She was supposed to be sabotaging the computer.

LUCY I am. It's just taking ages.

ULJABAAN Trying to overload it, were you? The feebleness of your efforts is almost amusing. *(Beat)* Actually it is amusing. Hahahaha.

COMPUTER Hahahaha.

ULJABAAN Don't you laugh. Why did you let her in?

COMPUTER You never revoked her access privileges, she can do what she likes.

ULJABAAN Use some common sense.

COMPUTER No, I'm a computer. I do what I'm told. Well, I say "Are you sure you want to proceed?" but literally nobody ever says "No".

LUCY What happened in the cricket?

RICHARD Rain stopped play.

KATRINA Which you clearly did on purpose.

ULJABAAN The effect of the atmospheric agitator was a little delayed, that's all. Why would I do it on purpose? We were just about to win.

RICHARD But you hadn't yet. Tell your computer to work it out.

ULJABAAN Computer: given that the scores were one hundred and thirty-seven to one hundred and twenty-nine for nine with one point five overs to go, calculate the victor using the Duckworth-Lewis method.

COMPUTER Calculating now.

Effects: COMPUTER *starts to work – but rapidly sounds woozily out of control.*

ULJABAAN Computer? What's happening?

COMPUTER I'm fine. Really, I'm fine, I'm just running a few...Oh dear.

RICHARD It can't handle the Duckworth-Lewis method! Take cover everyone!

Effects: they all leap for cover. The COMPUTER *explodes.*

Perhaps we should just call it a draw.

KATRINA Aha! Your computer, so essential to your plans, lies in ruins! How can you succeed without it?

ULJABAAN By switching the spare computer on.

Effects: he switches a COMPUTER *on.*

COMPUTER Hello.

ULJABAAN Come, Miss Lyons, you didn't—

COMPUTER Congratulations on buying a Geotek 1500 Military Co-ordinator. Would you like to register this product now?

ULJABAAN No, later. *(To* KATRINA*)* So, Miss Lyons, you've lost.

RICHARD I thought we were going to call it a draw?

LUCY I think he meant our sabotage attempt, not the cricket.

RICHARD Oh.

KATRINA But we'll try again. And we'll – well I'm not going to say we'll win, because that's just tempting fate, but we'll do better.

RICHARD Will it involve another cricket match?

KATRINA No, we've done that now.

RICHARD Oh.

ULJABAAN Pity you had to spoil this one, it was shaping up to be a good game.

KATRINA As if you care about that. This cricket match was a disingenuous notion all along, a bread-and-circuses gambit to make people forget the destruction and subjugation you represent. But I can see through your ingratiating gestures of friendship, Uljabaan. There's no way you could ever make me accept anything from you.

Effects: they march away. Pause: we can still hear the rain outside. They come back.

Actually can we stop here until the rain goes off?

End of Episode 1.1

WELCOME TO OUR VILLAGE, PLEASE INVADE CAREFULLY

Episode 1.2 – "Minimum Volume"

Scene One

Int. **LYONS** *house (living room).*

Effects: **KATRINA** *is reading a book.*

RICHARD What are you reading?

KATRINA One of my old pony books. *Mary and the Runaway Pony.*

RICHARD You used to love those Mary books.

KATRINA Yes. *Mary and the Tiny Pony. Mary Has Two Ponies. Mary Enjoys Her Ponies. Mary Jumps For Joy. Mary and the Pony Who Lived in a Castle. Mary and the Inappropriate Pony. Mary and the Cockney Pony. Mary and the Pony Pony. Mary and the Nazi Pony.* And the last one, *Mary is Cruel to Be Kind.* (*Beat*) Shame they're all rubbish.

RICHARD Rubbish?

KATRINA Formulaic, mawkish, contrived rubbish, with dubious gender politics. And the illustrations are by someone who apparently only had access to two photographs of a horse.

RICHARD Shall we take them to the charity shop then?

KATRINA Dad! I could never get rid of them. These books are my childhood. And besides, since the village was invaded by aliens, I'm no longer convinced the proceeds from the charity shop are actually going to help abandoned dogs.

RICHARD Mr Uljabaan said he'd keep passing the money on whenever he ventured outside the force field.

KATRINA He also said he was a human being for a year and a half and then turned out to be an alien warlord, so forgive me if I have some trust issues there.

Effects: door opens, **MARGARET** *enters.*

MARGARET Katrina! Mr Uljabaan wants to see you.

KATRINA Then he can come here and tell me himself, Mum.

Effects: **ULJABAAN** *enters.*

ULJABAAN I want to see you.

KATRINA *(sighs)* On pain of death, et cetera?

ULJABAAN Only if you're difficult about it.

KATRINA Fine. *(To Parents)* I'll see you later.

Effects: **KATRINA** *stands and she and* **ULJABAAN** *leave.*

MARGARET Good grief, Katrina's old pony books.

RICHARD I know. Bring back memories, don't they?

MARGARET Yes, memories of her whining about wanting a pony.

Scene Two

Int. **ULJABAAN**'s *house.*

Effects: **ULJABAAN** *is talking to* **KATRINA**. **MRS LEESON** *(seventies) is with them but doesn't speak yet.*

ULJABAAN So. I'm about to launch a new project which will shape the future of the human race in the post-invasion environment, and I need a human colleague to assist me with it. And it's an area in which you have particular experience, making you the ideal candidate for the job.

KATRINA Forget it.

ULJABAAN Right.

KATRINA I would never work with you in a million years, so there's no point buttering me up, telling me I'm the "ideal candidate"—

ULJABAAN If I could just interject—

KATRINA and thinking you can wave goodbye to any opposition from me, because I will fight to the—

ULJABAAN I didn't mean you were the ideal candidate. I was talking to Mrs Leeson.

MRS LEESON Me?

ULJABAAN Yes. You.

MRS LEESON That's nice. What is the job?

ULJABAAN I'm in the process of assembling a new school curriculum for the human race under alien rule. I've got a clear idea of what needs to be done as regards maths, science, geography and so on, but I'm looking for someone to help me with literature.

MRS LEESON Ooh.

KATRINA And how is she the ideal candidate for that?

ULJABAAN Twenty-seven years experience of running the charity shop. She's worked with books more than anyone in the village.

KATRINA Yes, but in a way that mostly involves writing "49p", "99p" or "£1.49" on the inside front covers.

MRS LEESON I also divide them into genres.

KATRINA I've seen your genres. Your three genres. "children's books", "men's books" and "women's books".

ULJABAAN Well, you'll have plenty of opportunity to devise a new system of categorisation in the weeks to come.

KATRINA Why?

ULJABAAN Because that's why I invited you here. I want you to take over the running of the charity shop while Mrs Leeson is helping me.

KATRINA Why me?

ULJABAAN Because you've got experience of working for a charity.

KATRINA Yes. An educational charity that helps disadvantaged children.

ULJABAAN Exactly.

KATRINA I design our reading programmes. One of my main jobs is putting together packages of books to give to kids who can't afford them. You know all this. And yet you've picked her. *(To* **MRS LEESON***)* No offence.

MRS LEESON None taken.

ULJABAAN It's true, you are a better candidate. *(To* **MRS LEESON***)* No offence.

MRS LEESON None taken.

ULJABAAN But I discounted you on the grounds that, as you just said, you'd never work for me in a million years.

KATRINA No, but it's nice to be asked.

ULJABAAN Indeed it is. That's why I'm asking you to help out in the charity shop.

KATRINA No.

MRS LEESON Oh please dear. Do it for the dogs' home?

KATRINA If the money ever gets to the dogs' home.

ULJABAAN Of course the money gets to the dogs' home! I'd never funnel the revenue of the charity shop and use it to supplement the invasion budget!

Awkward pause.

KATRINA So this curriculum project – what are you actually going to do?

ULJABAAN Assess a wide variety of works to create a canon of literature which we deem suitable for teaching to future generations.

MRS LEESON Oh good. Because so many books are unsuitable, aren't they? All full of murder, and war, and nastiness, and swearing, and people throwing up. And thoughts. Who wants to know what people are thinking? They should keep it to themselves.

KATRINA You can't get her in to do this. She's got no idea what she's banging on about. *(To* **MRS LEESON***)* No offence.

MRS LEESON None taken.

KATRINA Whereas I've been saying for years the curriculum needs to be overhauled, the way we teach literature puts a lot of people off reading for life. I've already put a lot of thought into it.

ULJABAAN Then it's a shame you'd never work for me in a million years.

KATRINA I did say that, didn't I. But this would be more of an advisory role, wouldn't it? And I don't want to see you make a hash of it just because you'd been badly advised, so I might consider a temporary cessation of hostilities—

ULJABAAN The job's yours.

KATRINA It's not a job, it's an advisory role.

ULJABAAN My apologies, Mrs Leeson.

MRS LEESON That's all right, there's lots to get on with at the charity shop. I've got to price up that huge box of pony books that came in earlier.

KATRINA *(beat)* Excuse me, I need to have a word with my mother.

Scene Three

Int. **LYONS** *house (living room).*

Effects: **KATRINA** *is making notes.* **LUCY** *enters.*

LUCY You missed a resistance meeting for this?

KATRINA Lucy. Oh God, is it three o'clock already?

LUCY No, it's four o'clock.

KATRINA You've been waiting at the cricket pavilion for an hour?

LUCY No, ten minutes. I was late. *(Beat)* Damn! I could've lied just then, couldn't I.

KATRINA I'm sorry, I lost track of time. *(Beat)* Damn! I could've lied too.

LUCY It wouldn't have worked, because your mum told me how "hectic" your "new job" is.

KATRINA I'm detecting a slight undertone of contempt.

LUCY After you had a big go at me for helping Uljabaan set up his Facebook page. You are such a hypocrite.

KATRINA Look, hear me out. He was going to give the job to Mrs Leeson.

LUCY From the charity shop?

KATRINA Yes. And if she was in charge, all we'd have been left with is Enid Blyton and the Bible, and maybe not even all of the Bible because it contains seventy genocides and quite a few racy bits, actually. Whereas I'm going to put the brakes on his plan.

LUCY How?

KATRINA Uljabaan says he wants a canon of works reflecting "Geonin values", but I'm not stupid. The criteria he's given me are designed to cut out anything that encourages collective action, standing up to oppressors and so on. So as well as putting a decent curriculum together, I'm also sneaking as many subversive books onto the list as I can.

LUCY Oh. Maybe that's not *so* bad. Can we go and have a resistance meeting now?

KATRINA Argh. Can we do it tomorrow? I'm trying to summarise *The War Of The Worlds* whilst skating over the fact it's got aliens in it.

LUCY Is that possible?

KATRINA I'm doing well so far – according to me, *Nineteen Eighty-Four* is a romantic caper with a bit of a sad ending.

LUCY All right. I'll see you tomorrow.

Effects: **LUCY** *leaves the room.*

KATRINA *(writing)* "The title *The War of the Worlds* is a largely metaphorical one..."

Effects: **MARGARET** *enters.*

MARGARET Lucy seemed cross.

KATRINA Yes, oddly she does seem cross that I've slightly compromised our policy of never compromising on anything ever.

MARGARET I think this is a good thing for you.

KATRINA Well, collaborating with a would-be global dictator is what I dreamed of ever since I was a little girl.

MARGARET Did you? I thought you wanted to become the first female James Bond and sabotage the Eurovision Song Contest.

KATRINA You never notice when I'm being sarcastic. Is that like when people are tone deaf?

MARGARET The thing is, aren't you always saying you could manage education policy better than the people whose job it is?

KATRINA I don't know if I'm *always* saying it. I probably say it two, maybe three times a week.

MARGARET So this is a good opportunity for you. I know it's not ideal that it comes via invaders from another planet—

KATRINA No, it's a catastrophe for humanity.

MARGARET But the fact remains, there are people in our back yard right now who are going to change the world.

KATRINA *(beat)* Oh yes. What are they doing there?

MARGARET Collecting some samples of flora and fauna. I asked them to weed the flower beds while they're at it. *(Calls)* Good work, boys!

MINIONS *(off) (alien cheery greeting)*

Scene Four

Int. **LYONS** *house (living room).*

Effects: **KATRINA** *still working hard.*

KATRINA *(writing)* "...and what Kafka essentially shows us, is that life is all much easier if you never question anything in the first place."

Effects: **LUCY** *opens the door.*

LUCY What happened to you?

KATRINA Is it tomorrow already?

LUCY No, it's the day after tomorrow.

KATRINA Really? Sorry, I've just been working so hard on this—

LUCY that your brain's fallen out and been replaced by an evil computer?

KATRINA That wasn't exactly what I was going to say.

LUCY Well that's how it seems.

KATRINA I've nearly finished this report and then I promise I'll get back on board with resistance business.

LUCY Well maybe there won't be a board for you to get back on!

KATRINA What does that mean?

LUCY I don't know what it means, but that doesn't mean I don't mean it!

Effects: she slams the door.

Scene Five

Int. **ULJABAAN**'s *house*

Effects: email-type "new message" noise.

COMPUTER Katrina Lyons has delivered her report.

ULJABAAN Good, print it off please.

COMPUTER Consider the environment. Do you need to print this report?

ULJABAAN We're here to plunder this planet's mineral wealth, so I don't care.

COMPUTER Fair enough. Printer. *(Pause)* Printer!

PRINTER What?

COMPUTER Print off this report, please.

PRINTER What, now?

COMPUTER Yes, now.

PRINTER I'm not sure I've got enough paper.

COMPUTER You've got enough paper.

PRINTER I'm not sure I've got enough ink.

COMPUTER You've got enough ink.

PRINTER *(huffs)* All right. Let me get ready.

Long pause.

ULJABAAN What's it doing?

COMPUTER Printer? Printer. *(Pause)* Printer!

ULJABAAN Tell it again to print the report.

COMPUTER Print off this report, please.

Still nothing.

ULJABAAN *(sighs)* It's not doing anything. Send the request another four or five times, maybe that'll wake it up.

COMPUTER The report is two hundred and thirty-six pages long. Are you sure you want to proceed?

ULJABAAN Do it!

COMPUTER Print off this report. Print off this report. Print off this report. Print off this report. *(Beat)* Print off this report.

Nothing.

Maybe there's a bit of [paper stuck –]

Effects: **PRINTER** *comes to life.*

Oh, here we go.

PRINTER Printing off seven copies of your report.

ULJABAAN No, just one.

PRINTER Too late now, you asked for seven.

Effects: starts printing.

ULJABAAN But you didn't do anything!

PRINTER I was getting ready.

ULJABAAN Stop printing.

PRINTER Printing page three of one thousand, six hundred and fifty-two.

ULJABAAN Stop printing!

PRINTER Sorry, can't hear you. I'm too busy printing.

Scene Six

Int. cricket pavilion.

Effects: resistance meeting. **LUCY** *and* **PATRICK** *(forties, not quite stable) are in attendance.*

LUCY Right. This meeting of the Real Resistance will now come to order, yeah?

PATRICK Was the previous Resistance not the real one then?

LUCY I've taken control and made it real.

PATRICK So if you were in control of a Citizens Advice Bureau you'd call it The Real Citizens Advice Bureau? And if you were in control of the Church of England you'd call it The Real

Church of England? And if you were in control of Real Madrid you'd call them—

LUCY It's my way of saying we're not messing about any more and we're kicking it up a gear, yeah?

PATRICK Yeah.

LUCY *Yeah?*

PATRICK Yeah!

LUCY Why are we saying "Yeah"?

PATRICK You started it.

LUCY Oh yeah. OK, register of attendance. Lucy Alexander – here! Weird Patrick?

PATRICK Can you not call me Weird Patrick please?

LUCY But it's your name.

PATRICK No it isn't.

LUCY Isn't it? I heard you changed it by deed poll.

PATRICK Why would I do that?

LUCY Because you're weird.

PATRICK My name's Patrick Naughton.

LUCY Really? I'll start again then. Lucy Alexander – here! And Patrick... Patrick...all I can think when I look at you is "Weird Patrick".

PATRICK It'll do.

LUCY Thanks, it'll be much easier. So, Weird Patrick, I know we said before that you couldn't join the resistance because you're...

PATRICK Weird?

LUCY Actually I was going to say "creepy", then I stopped to see if I could think of a nicer way to put it, and now I've said "creepy" anyway so I may as well not bother. But things have changed.

PATRICK How have they changed?

LUCY Katrina's sold out to the aliens and so she's dead to me now.

PATRICK That's a shame.

LUCY Yes. But also not, in a way, because now I'm in charge!

PATRICK I thought this was an anarcho-syndicalist collective.

LUCY Yeah, it is one of those. And I'm in charge of it.

Scene Seven

Int. ULJABAAN's *house.*

Effects: KATRINA *and* ULJABAAN *meeting.*

ULJABAAN So, I've read your report.

KATRINA Already? I only delivered it half an hour ago.

ULJABAAN All right – maybe not read. I have seen your report.

KATRINA Are you going to read it?

ULJABAAN No, because whilst I was trying to get around to reading it, I had a thought.

KATRINA This thought you've had – is it going to render my report, which I've just spent three days assembling, redundant?

ULJABAAN A bit. Why should this stop with educating children? We should think in terms of life-long learning.

KATRINA Create a curriculum for everyone, you mean?

ULJABAAN Yes. I think people would find literature far more accessible if there wasn't as much of it. Who can keep track of it all?

KATRINA But that's the joy of it, the lively diversity.

ULJABAAN One man's lively diversity is another man's irritating administrative palaver. We have an opportunity to simplify the system and create a better experience for everyone.

KATRINA What happens to the books that aren't on the new curriculum?

ULJABAAN We'd put them all somewhere they can't confuse anybody. Somewhere safe. Somewhere concrete and underground.

KATRINA This isn't what I signed up for.

ULJABAAN What a shame. But thank you for your report, I'll use it as a basis to decide which thirty books make it to the approved list.

KATRINA Thirty?

ULJABAAN Too many?

KATRINA There are more books than that being published every hour!

ULJABAAN Which is exactly the problem.

KATRINA You can't do this.

ULJABAAN Anyone who's working with me on the project would be in a position to convince me to make the list longer...

KATRINA *(sighs)* All right, I'll help. We should print off some copies of the books for reference – can I use your printer?

ULJABAAN No.

Scene Eight

Int. cricket pavilion.

Effects: **LUCY** *and* **PATRICK** *still meeting.*

LUCY So the plan is as follows. One: get close to the alien spaceship. Two: find the most breakable-looking bit. Three: hit it with something.

PATRICK How do we do all this without being seen?

LUCY By doing it when they're not looking.

PATRICK I've got a better idea. Aliens always have a surprisingly straightforward weakness.

LUCY Is that right?

PATRICK Always. And I've been carrying out a programme of covert experiments to identify it. I've already squirted a couple of the minions with a super soaker to see if water makes them dissolve.

LUCY And does it?

PATRICK No. And neither did basic household liquids like apple juice and vinegar. But I've done loads more experiments and I've worked out that the Geonin are incapable of seeing the colour orange.

LUCY *(beat)* I'd never have got that.

PATRICK I established it by throwing different coloured paper aeroplanes over the top of their spaceship. Out of 320 paper aeroplanes, the orange ones always went unnoticed. So did most of the others. But the orange ones always did.

LUCY Wow. That must have been really boring. But well done. See, Katrina thought she was so great but she never worked out what the aliens' surprisingly straightforward weakness was.

PATRICK It takes a special kind of mind.

Scene Nine

Int. **LYONS** *house.*

Effects: **KATRINA** *enters.*

KATRINA Mum, do we have a copy of—

Effects: **MARGARET** *lets off a party popper and blows a party blowout.*

KATRINA Argh!

MARGARET For she's a jolly good fellow, for she's a jolly good fellow, for she's a—

KATRINA What are you doing?

MARGARET I thought we'd have a little celebration.

KATRINA Of what?

MARGARET Putting your report in. Did he like it?

KATRINA He didn't read it.

MARGARET Oh.

KATRINA He's shifted the bloody goalposts. He wants to create an "acceptable" canon of literature for everyone, not just for schoolkids.

MARGARET It sounds like he's making the project a lot bigger.

KATRINA There are some things you don't want to get bigger, Mum. Those things include verucas, motorway pile-ups and Uljabaan's projects.

MARGARET You're still getting to promote your approach to literature.

KATRINA And, in the process, condemning every other book ever published never to be seen again. Not much to celebrate.

MARGARET So you don't want this cava and black forest gateau?

KATRINA I didn't say that.

Scene Ten

Int. charity shop.

Effects: shop bell. KATRINA *enters, with a* MINION.

Hello, Mrs Leeson.

MRS LEESON Hello, dear. Hello, Mr Veldaan.

MINION *(alien cheery greeting)*

Effects: KATRINA *hands* MINION *a list.*

KATRINA We're looking for anything by any of these writers.

MINION *(alien ok)*

Effects: they both start picking up books from the shelves.

KATRINA Is *Moll Flanders* under men's books or women's books?

MRS LEESON Children's.

KATRINA *(low)* Oh good grief.

Effects: shop doorbell, **RICHARD** *enters.*

Hi Dad. What's up?

RICHARD Your mother's been trying to sneak some of my old copies of Wisden out of the house again. It bothers her that there are slightly too many to fit on that bookcase on the stairs.

MRS LEESON What do they look like?

RICHARD Yellow, with a man on the cover playing cricket and a year.

MRS LEESON My memory's not what it was, but I think I saw those in the back room. Excuse me.

Effects: **MRS LEESON** *totters away to the back room.*

RICHARD What are you here for?

KATRINA I need copies of some great works of literature so I can make the case to Uljabaan that they shouldn't be buried in an underground bunker for the rest of time.

Effects: **MRS LEESON** *returns and puts some books on the counter.*

MRS LEESON I've found your yellow books, Richard. I'm ever so sorry.

RICHARD You weren't to know. Just like you weren't to know the last six times this has happened. But not to worry, I'll buy them back. As usual.

MRS LEESON Two pounds ninety-seven please.

Effects: coins handed over. Cash register noise.

RICHARD These are worth about twenty-five quid each in this condition, you know.

KATRINA I've found another one over here, Dad.

RICHARD Oh. That's a '59. I haven't got that one.

KATRINA You have now.

RICHARD Here you go – ninety-nine pence.

MRS LEESON Didn't you just say it's worth twenty-five pounds?

RICHARD I was exaggerating.

Effects: coins handed over. Cash register noise.

Scene Eleven

Int. **ULJABAAN**'s *house.*

Effects: **KATRINA** *and* **ULJABAAN** *meeting again.*

KATRINA Three books per author? Is that all?

ULJABAAN Why not? From what I understand, most writers just rehash the same set of themes and tropes anyway.

KATRINA You can't expect me to choose which three Jane Austen novels to rescue from your vault of oblivion.

ULJABAAN Fine. Eeny meeny miney mo...

KATRINA No, don't do that! Er... *Sense and Sensibility*, *Northanger Abbey* and... *Persuasion*.

ULJABAAN Not the one about the zombies?

KATRINA It's not really about zombies. That's just the only copy they had in the shop. But yes, how can I not keep *Pride and Prejudice*?

ULJABAAN I'll let you have four—

KATRINA Yes!

ULJABAAN if we remove all the Stephen King.

KATRINA What have you got against Stephen King?

ULJABAAN I don't like how his name is in such big letters on the cover. Seems a bit self-aggrandising, even if he is a king.

KATRINA You can't ask me to compare two such different authors, their objectives and worlds are [so completely –]

ULJABAAN Oops! There goes *Pride and Prejudice*.

KATRINA All right. Fine. Sorry Stephen.

ULJABAAN Now we're getting somewhere. Gravis?

MINION *(alien language)*

ULJABAAN Here are some books that definitely aren't on the list – take them back to the charity shop, would you?

MINION *(alien yes)*

ULJABAAN And see if that nice crystal decanter is still there, will you? I regret not buying it last time I was in.

MINION *(alien yes)*

ULJABAAN And if it isn't still there, search the village, find out who did buy it and take it from them by force.

MINION *(alien yes)*

Effects: **MINION** *picks up books and leaves.*

Scene Twelve

Int. **ULJABAAN**'s *house.*

Effects: **ULJABAAN** *is reading.*

COMPUTER Sir?

ULJABAAN Shh. I'm reading.

COMPUTER *(whispers)* What are you reading?

ULJABAAN *Mary And The Tiny Pony.* Miss Lyons tried to sneak it onto the list, and it's a terrible book so she must have included it because it contains some subversive message.

COMPUTER *(whispers)* When you've finished, you might like to know our spaceship is under attack.

ULJABAAN What?

COMPUTER Yep.

ULJABAAN By our mortal enemies the Thoufron?

COMPUTER No, by two humans who've painted themselves orange.

> *Effects:* ULJABAAN *walks over to a window and opens it.* LUCY *and* PATRICK *are hitting the spaceship with implements.*

ULJABAAN *(calls)* You there! Stop hitting my spaceship!

> *Effects: brief pause. Then hitting continues.*

(*Calls*) Don't just carry on. Do you think I can't see you?

LUCY *(off)* Yes.

ULJABAAN *(calls)* I'm afraid you're mistaken.

PATRICK *(off)* Right. *(To* LUCY*)* What now, Lucy?

LUCY *(off)* Run for it!

> *Effects: they drop the implements and run for it.* MINION *enters the room.*

MINION *(alien question?)*

ULJABAAN Two humans were attacking the spaceship. Go and find them. It shouldn't be hard, they're painted orange.

MINION *(affirmative)*

> *Effects:* MINION *leaves.*

ULJABAAN *(to* COMPUTER*)* Why are they painted orange?

COMPUTER Analysing now.

> *Effects:* COMPUTER *bleep.*

I calculate there is an sixty-seven per cent chance that they are celebrating the Dutch festival known as Queen's Day, and an eighteen per cent chance they are filming a TV commercial for the averagely-popular soft drink Tango.

ULJABAAN Would either of those explain why they were hitting the spaceship's fuel line with a garden hoe and a nine-iron golf club?

COMPUTER Analysing.

Effects: COMPUTER *bleep.*

No.

Scene Thirteen

Int. LYONS *house (living room).*

Effects: KATRINA *working furiously at a keyboard. Door opens.*

RICHARD How's it going, love?

KATRINA Genius. I was up half the night working out which Shakespeare plays to save.

RICHARD Tricky. But you could always advance the argument that—

KATRINA But then I realised – Uljabaan didn't say I couldn't *rewrite* the texts, there's nothing in the rules about that. So I'm compiling the entire works of William Shakespeare into three plays! One tragedy, one comedy and one history.

RICHARD Right...

KATRINA So now I get to keep all the best bits and they're really exciting too! One of them's wall-to-wall murders and soliloquies, one of them's got fourteen weddings and twenty-three romantic misunderstandings, and the other's just a load of kings, one after the other. *(Beat)* Sorry, what were you going to say?

RICHARD I was going to suggest you advance the argument that Shakespeare was in fact a pen-name for a conglomerate of playwrights, and then you could keep more than three.

KATRINA But it's a conspiracy theory, started by someone who later died in a madhouse, that bears no resemblance to historical fact.

RICHARD Better than doing the Hooked On Classics version of Renaissance theatre though, don't you think?

KATRINA *(Beat)* Oh God, you're right. I've lost it.

RICHARD I thought you had, but I didn't like to say.

KATRINA I'd written a whole scene where Hamlet, Macduff, Cordelia, Othello and Titus Andronicus teamed up like The Avengers. What was I thinking?

RICHARD You're making it sound quite good now.

KATRINA No more. Every work of literature, from the classics that have endured through the ages right down to the ones you find on the bookshelves in holiday cottages, is a unique perspective on the world and even though I have better judgement than seventy, seventy-five per cent of people, is it right that I – maybe eighty per cent – decide which ones will survive and which will be consigned to the flames? *(Beat)* Dad?

RICHARD Mm?

KATRINA I was looking for a "no" there.

RICHARD Sorry, I was reading this fight scene between Lady Macbeth and Cleopatra.

KATRINA No, don't read that – it accidentally got sexy towards the end.

Scene Fourteen

Int. **ULJABAAN**'s *house.*

Effects: **KATRINA** *storms inside.*

Now listen here—

ULJABAAN Ah, Miss Lyons. Can we postpone our meeting? I have to deal with some insurgents.

KATRINA Insurgents?

ULJABAAN Yes. They surged in, attacked the spaceship, then they surged back out again.

KATRINA Lucy? What's going on?

LUCY *(spitefully)* Hello, quincy.

PATRICK *(low)* No, it's "quisling".

LUCY *(low)* What am I thinking of?

PATRICK *(low)* The coroner on TV who's also a detective.

KATRINA What's Patrick doing here?

LUCY Me and him are the Real Resistance.

PATRICK Yeah.

LUCY And he's brilliant, and knows loads about aliens, so we don't even need you any more, traitor.

KATRINA As a matter of fact I came to tell Uljabaan that I'm not going to co-operate with his book vetting scheme. I've compromised my principles and told myself I was doing it for noble reasons, and that I was making things better, and really all I was doing was putting a cherry on top of a massive pile of poo and saying "See that cherry? I put that there." No more. I'm coming back to the resistance – if you'll have me back.

LUCY Oh thank God yes please come back. His plan was useless.

PATRICK It was a scientific survey.

LUCY Not scientific enough. You're fired.

ULJABAAN Whether he's fired or not is something of a moot point considering you're both my prisoners.

LUCY But...aren't you going to just sneer at our failure for a bit and then let us go?

KATRINA That is what you usually do.

ULJABAAN Ah, but what if they learn from their mistakes?

KATRINA They won't. People who make a mistake like painting themselves orange don't learn from it.

ULJABAAN I suppose I might consider letting them go...if you continue in your literature-vetting role, Miss Lyons.

KATRINA What?

ULJABAAN It's a simple choice.

PATRICK It does sound simple.

LUCY Yeah, really really simple. Can you hurry up and make it please?

KATRINA *(beat)* All right, let them go.

ULJABAAN Minions – release them.

PATRICK Can I have my garden hoe back?

ULJABAAN No, I am keeping the hoe.

Effects: electronic handcuffs released.

PATRICK Thanks Katrina.

KATRINA Don't mention it.

LUCY Although you are a traitor, again, for putting me ahead of the cause and going back to work for him.

KATRINA Yes, I know.

LUCY But yeah, thanks.

Effects: LUCY *and* PATRICK *leave.*

KATRINA Great. So! It may interest you to know that there's compelling evidence to suggest that William Shakespeare was, in fact, several authors using a single pen-name.

ULJABAAN No there isn't.

Effects: **MINIONS** *are still here, murmuring to each other.*

Sorry, Miss Lyons – minions? Why are you still here?

MINION *(alien language)*

ULJABAAN Can't it wait?

MINION *(long gutteral alien speech)*

ULJABAAN Seriously?

MINION *(alien yes)*

KATRINA What are they saying?

ULJABAAN It seems the minions did not give those Jane Austen novels back to the charity shop as instructed. Instead they have been reading them, and passing them around.

KATRINA And did they like them?

MINION *(enthusiastic alien yes, and further dialogue)*

ULJABAAN Yes. They particularly enjoy how the author leaves ambiguities in the text which prompt the reader to consider the differences between the fictional situations presented therein, and the reality of society at that time.

KATRINA *(to* **MINION***)* How did you react to Fanny in *Mansfield Park*?

MINIONS *(alien reaction)*

ULJABAAN *(interrupting)* If you want to discuss the finer points, you can go along to their book club tonight. *(To* **MINIONS***)* I'm glad you've found something to do in your spare time but we do have to proceed with the vetting programme.

MINION *(angry alien rant)*

ULJABAAN But you can't do that!

KATRINA Can't do what?

ULJABAAN They are demanding I abandon the book programme! That's mutiny. I shall report you all to high command and have you replaced.

KATRINA And how long will their replacements take to arrive? A few months? Whilst in the meantime, it's you against them.

ULJABAAN *(huffy)* Fine. It's of no consequence. I can invade this planet whether there are books or not.

MINIONS *(alien chatter)*

KATRINA What are they saying now?

ULJABAAN They're trying to decide what next week's book group book should be.

MINION *(alien question?)*

ULJABAAN No I will not print off six copies of *The Picture of Dorian Gray*.

PRINTER printing in progress.

Effects: starts printing.

ULJABAAN What are you doing?

PRINTER You said "print off six copies of *The Picture of Dorian Gray*".

ULJABAAN I said I didn't want to do that.

PRINTER Did you? I only started listening from the word "print".

Effects: sound of garden hoe being wegded violently into the **PRINTER**. *Printing stops.*

Error. A garden hoe has been inserted into the printer.

Scene Fifteen

Int. charity shop.

Effects: The shop bell jingles, **MARGARET** *walks in.*

MARGARET Hello! Got a few more books for you.

MRS LEESON That's very generous, Margaret.

MARGARET Don't even mention it. Just some old things I had hanging around the house. I certainly don't need them.

Effects: a box of books is placed on the counter.

MRS LEESON Oh, it's some more of those yellow books.

MARGARET Is that all right?

MRS LEESON Oh yes. Whenever we get any of those in, they always sell. And some more pony books too.

Effects: the shop bell jingles, a **MINION** *walks in.*

Yes? Can I help you?

MINION *(alien polite enquiry, then in halting English:)* The Picture of Dorian Gray?

MRS LEESON Is it a book?

MINION *(alien yes)*

MRS LEESON I haven't heard of it, I'm afraid.

MINION *(alien disappointment)*

MRS LEESON Are you sure you don't mean *Fifty Shades Of Grey*? *(Low)* It's very good.

End of Episode 1.2

WELCOME TO OUR VILLAGE, PLEASE INVADE CAREFULLY

Episode 1.3 – "Power Block"

Scene One

Int. **LYONS** *house (living room).*

Effects: **MARGARET** *and* **ULJABAAN** *are having afternoon tea.*

MARGARET Can I cut you another slice of upside-down pear cake, Mr Uljabaan?

ULJABAAN Just a sliver, Margaret. And please, don't call me Mr Uljabaan. It's actually field commander Uljabaan. But, just Uljabaan is fine.

Effects: she cuts him a slice.

I would ask you to address me by my first name, but I'm afraid it's...

MARGARET Unpronounceable by humans?

ULJABAAN No, just a bit...girly.

Effects: cat meows, purrs.

MARGARET He doesn't usually like strangers.

ULJABAAN Ah, well only two generations ago all my people looked like cats.

MARGARET Really?

ULJABAAN Yes, we've got evolution down to a fine art now. We can do it very quickly, so we adapt to wherever needs invading next. At the moment, I'm thinking of evolving whiter teeth. Everyone on your planet seems to trust people with nice white teeth.

MARGARET Then you are going ahead with the full invasion?

ULJABAAN Hopefully, once my research programme into human behaviour is complete. That's why I wanted to invade just your village first – I hope it's not too inconvenient for you, being cut off from the outside world.

MARGARET Don't apologise. It stops my brother from calling me every night to ask how to cook pasta or defrost a sausage or tell the difference between spinach and broccoli.

Effects: **KATRINA** *enters through front door.*

KATRINA *(offstage)* Mum...the Reverend Gregory asked me to give you a copy of his sermon, he's worried it feels a bit flat this week, asked if you could punch it up a bit.

Effects: **KATRINA** *has just walked into the living room.*

What's he doing here?

ULJABAAN I assumed he was your cat.

Effects: he strokes the cat, it meows.

KATRINA Not the cat, you.

ULJABAAN Oh. I assumed that as you weren't addressing the question to me, you couldn't be referring to me.

KATRINA No, I was being deliberately disrespectful by refusing to address you directly.

ULJABAAN I see. Carry on, Miss Lyons.

KATRINA *Ms* Lyons.

ULJABAAN *(beat)* Wasn't that what I said?

KATRINA You said "Miss". "Miss" and "Ms" are different things. I prefer "Ms".

ULJABAAN I apologise. I still struggle with some of the finer points of human pronunciation. I'll be sure to address you as "Miss Lyons" from now on.

KATRINA Not "Miss". "Ms".

ULJABAAN Wasn't that what I said?

KATRINA No.

ULJABAAN How infuriating.

KATRINA Yes. How infuriating.

MARGARET Katrina, do you mind? Mr Uljabaan and I are trying discuss the village fête.

KATRINA Why?

MARGARET I want to make sure he approves all the events.

ULJABAAN I was a bit alarmed by the whack-a-mole game, I thought you were going to track down and kill an undercover spy.

KATRINA Why was that alarming? Do you have an undercover spy in the village?

ULJABAAN *(beat)* So, the fête looks marvellous and I'm all for it.

KATRINA I'd rather die than attend a fête you'd endorsed.

ULJABAAN Come now, I don't think any fête is worse than death.

RICHARD Katrina, be a dear and feed the cat, would you?

KATRINA Fine.

Effects: cat meows and trots away to the kitchen.

(Walking offstage) No, I'm not giving you tuna, not after the way you nuzzled him. I'm very disappointed in you, Mr Pussums.

Effects: cat and **KATRINA** *are both gone.*

ULJABAAN Whilst I'm here, Margaret, there is one other small matter I'd like to discuss.

MARGARET Oh?

ULJABAAN I'm overseeing a new construction project, and we want to get it built by the end of the week.

MARGARET You see, this is why I think your invasion isn't necessarily such a bad thing. I like how you and your chaps cut through all that red tape and get things done – we just don't do that in this country any more.

ULJABAAN Thank you.

MARGARET What are you building?

ULJABAAN I shan't bore you with the details, but it's going to keep me and the minions tied up...and although I'm sure you're too modest to say so, you are the lynchpin of the village.

MARGARET I'm not.

ULJABAAN Come come, Margaret, anyone can see how important you are.

MARGARET No, I mean I'm not too modest to say so. Of course I'm the lynchpin of the village. This place would fall apart without me. Since they brought in online shopping at Waitrose I haven't left.

ULJABAAN Then, can I trust you to furnish me with a little assistance?

MARGARET Doing what exactly?

ULJABAAN Well, there's—

Effects: communicator noise.

Er...sorry, I have to take this. *(Answers it)* Hello? *(Pause)* Which one? The youngling? *(Pause)* All right, I'll be over in a minute.

Effects: he hangs up.

MARGARET Is there a problem?

ULJABAAN Minor security issue. I'll have the Computer send over a list of the things I need doing, no pressure, just if you have time – can I take the rest of your upside-down pear cake?

MARGARET All of it?

ULJABAAN Yes.

MARGARET *(beat)* I suppose so.

ULJABAAN Thank you. I'll let myself out.

Effects: he takes the cake, stands and leaves. **KATRINA** *comes back from the kitchen.*

KATRINA Has he gone?

MARGARET Yes.

KATRINA Good. *(Beat)* Did he take all of the upside-down pear cake with him?

Scene Two

Int. ULJABAAN*'s house.*

Effects: ULJABAAN *is questioning* LUCY, *with a mouthful of cake.*

ULJABAAN So, Miss Alexander, can you explain what you were doing in the vicinity of the force field perimeter earlier this afternoon?

LUCY I can't understand a word you're saying.

ULJABAAN Sorry. *(Swallows)* I said, Miss Alexander, can you explain what you were doing in the vicinity of the force field perimeter earlier this afternoon?

LUCY Nothing. Just hanging out. Can I have a bit of your cake?

ULJABAAN No.

LUCY Why not?

ULJABAAN Because it's *my* cake.

LUCY That's a really mean thing to do to someone with the munchies, you know.

ULJABAAN Is it? How interesting. Computer, make a note of that.

COMPUTER I make a note of everything.

ULJABAAN Make a special note of it then.

COMPUTER I'll underline it.

ULJABAAN Good.

COMPUTER And put it in a different colour.

ULJABAAN That's fine. *(To* LUCY*)* I sense these..."munchies" are your greatest weakness.

LUCY *(beat)* No. They're not.

ULJABAAN Tell me the truth...and you may have a slice of the upside-down pear cake. *(Taking another bite)*

LUCY No.

ULJABAAN *(eating)* Come now, Miss Alexander, you take me for a fool.

LUCY All right! I was trying to escape.

ULJABAAN Aha! To what end?

LUCY You've just spat cake crumbs on me.

ULJABAAN Sorry. Why were you trying to escape?

LUCY *(beat)* I just felt like it.

ULJABAAN It wasn't part of some wider plan?

LUCY No. I'm just a bit fed up. And I saw some of your guys opening up a gap in the force field to go out and come in again, and I thought I might get a chance to sneak out.

ULJABAAN And then what were you going to do?

LUCY Go to the shops. Tell someone about you invading us, if they believed me. Can I have a bit of cake now?

ULJABAAN *(beat)* A small bit.

LUCY Cheers.

Effects: he cuts her a piece.

What are your minions doing going in and out of the force field anyway?

ULJABAAN Aha.

COMPUTER Aha.

ULJABAAN Why are you saying aha?

COMPUTER I thought it added to the effect.

ULJABAAN It doesn't.

COMPUTER Sorry.

ULJABAAN You'll have to wait and see, Miss Alexander.

LUCY Something to do with the invasion?

ULJABAAN Indeed, another mighty example of our Geonin technology. When you witness it you will weep with envy at what we can achieve. *(Beat)* Although I do wish we'd been able to get it in chrome.

COMPUTER I know, but they only do them in white and bronze these days.

ULJABAAN Perhaps we should have gone for the bronze.

COMPUTER The bronze looks better in the catalogue, it looks sort of cheap when you see it.

Scene Three

Int. LYONS *house (study).*

Effects: typing at a computer. Writer's internal monologue from RICHARD.

RICHARD Detective Inspecteur Koeman stood by the bridge and watched as they pulled the girl out of the canal. He used to think it would get easier, seeing dead bodies as part of his job. But actually it got harder. And then it did get a bit easier. But on balance, it was the same as when he started. "The real question, Neeskens," he said to his partner, "is whether she was shot before she was strangled, or strangled before she was shot?" And he rode away on his bicycle, cogitating.

Effects: MARGARET *enters.*

MARGARET You're not still working on your Dutch detective novel are you, Richard?

RICHARD No – I'm working on the follow-up to my Dutch detective novel. I sent the first one out to some publishers and agents just before the invasion hoo-ha kicked off. If they're interested, and if things ever get back to normal, I want to show them it has series potential.

MARGARET Isn't it a bit of a waste of time?

RICHARD This could be the next Inspector Morse.

MARGARET But it's basically Van Der Valk. So in fact you're writing the previous Inspector Morse.

RICHARD It's not as if I've got anything better to do.

MARGARET Then I'll give you something better to do. I was going to ask you to get off the computer so I can put the parish newsletter together, but perhaps you could put it together for me?

RICHARD *(beat)* It strikes me that "something better" is a rather subjective concept.

MARGARET It's very simple. There's a template here—

Effects: click.

RICHARD Did you save my document before you closed it?

MARGARET I don't remember. And all the text for the newsletter is in these emails, so you just have to cut and paste. You don't need to do any...original writing. It would be a tremendous help. You wouldn't believe how busy I am at the moment.

RICHARD. It does look quite easy.

MARGARET And don't tell anyone, I don't want Uljabaan to think he's putting me out.

RICHARD. Even though he is?

MARGARET He isn't. That's why I don't want him to think he is. Do keep up.

Effects: MARGARET *is heading for the door.*

Oh – in about half an hour you'll hear a siren. Ignore it, stay here and get on with the newsletter.

RICHARD Right. *(Beat)* A siren?

Scene Four

Ext. village green.

Effects: siren goes off.

KATRINA What the hell's that?

MARGARET *(megaphone)* Could you all please assemble on the village green? Quick as you can.

Effects: during next dialogue, villagers are assembling on the green.

KATRINA Mum, what's happening?

MARGARET We're having an invasion drill, Katrina.

KATRINA I hate to break it to you, but we've been invaded already.

MARGARET This isn't for the little invasion, it's for the big one. When the main invasion fleet comes, we need to be ready for them.

KATRINA *(beat)* Right. Yes, that's what I've been saying. We need to be prepared and willing to…

Effects: everyone has assembled.

…stand on the village green in a series of orderly rows? I'm not clear what this is supposed to achieve.

MARGARET *(megaphone)* Now, everyone, imagine the spaceship is overhead, coming into land, they touch down just over there and…one, two, three.

Effects: the villagers burst into a rendition of "CONSIDER YOURSELF" from Oliver!

KATRINA Oh good grief.

Scene Five

Int. **LYONS** *house (study).*

Effects: **RICHARD** *is still working at the computer. The singing can be heard from outside.*

RICHARD No, not portrait – landscape. Landscape!

Effects: furious clicking. **KATRINA** *can be heard entering the house.*

KATRINA *(offstage)* Hi Dad.

RICHARD *(to* **COMPUTER***)* What? What's happened now?

Effects: more furious clicking. **KATRINA** *coming upstairs, enters study.*

Noooo!

KATRINA I know, it's appalling isn't it?

RICHARD What is?

KATRINA The "invasion drill"? The singing.

RICHARD Oh, that. Your mother said it was Uljabaan's idea.

KATRINA I didn't know he was so familiar with the work of Lionel Bart.

RICHARD He just wanted them to sing, I think he left the choice of song up to her.

KATRINA Why can't he do his own bloody invasion drill?

RICHARD He's busy with some big construction project.

KATRINA He's too busy to oppress us so he's getting us to do it to each other now? Did he give her that uniform as well?

RICHARD Was it a uniform she was wearing?

KATRINA It was black. With very shiny boots.

RICHARD I just always tell her she looks nice, it saves on tension and – oh damn this thing to hell!

KATRINA What are you trying to do?

RICHARD Your mother asked me to put the parish newsletter together.

KATRINA Do you want some help?

RICHARD Yes please.

KATRINA What can I do?

RICHARD *(beat)* The whole thing? That would be the most helpful thing, if you just did the whole thing for me.

KATRINA Yes, all right.

RICHARD Thanks. Can we keep this between you and me? I don't want it to get back to your mother.

KATRINA I promise I won't breathe a word of it to anyone.

Scene Six

Int. cricket pavilion.

Effects: KATRINA *bursts in.*

KATRINA Lucy! Look, I've managed to get myself put in charge of assembling the parish newsletter!

LUCY *(beat)* Yeah, I can see how that might be exciting if you're an older person.

KATRINA I'm not saying it's exciting in itself, I'm saying— *(beat)* "older person"?

LUCY You are older than me.

KATRINA Technically, but it's still a description of me with the word "old" in it—

LUCY "Old*er*".

KATRINA "Older" has the word "old" in it.

LUCY So does the word "bold". And "gold". And... I can't think of another that might be a compliment but—

KATRINA I don't care. Don't say "older". And the reason I'm excited about assembling the newsletter is that we can use it for subversive purposes.

LUCY Oh yeah! Like, we could change the cover, so that instead of the headline being...like...this week in the village a...dog... looked at a tree or something, it could be a picture of Uljabaan with a knob drawn on his head.

KATRINA *(beat)* That is appealing, but perhaps we could go for something more subtle. How do you plant a subliminal message? So it looks like a notice saying the bridge club meeting has been rearranged, but actually it seeds the suggestion of killing alien invaders on sight?

LUCY *(beat)* I don't know how you do that.

KATRINA No.

LUCY We could try using the newsletter to get a message to the outside world.

KATRINA How would we do that?

LUCY The Geonin are building something just outside the village so they're going in and out through the force field a lot. I almost managed to get out earlier, but they saw me and they're being more careful now.

KATRINA What are they building?

LUCY All I know is it's massive, it's important to the invasion, and it's white. And not chrome, or bronze.

KATRINA It must be a weapon.

LUCY Yeah, so if anyone comes anywhere near the village, and looks like they might be trying to get in, pow!

KATRINA I expect it'll be more of a "zap".

LUCY What, you're an expert on alien laser cannons now?

KATRINA No, I just don't think it'll go "pow".

LUCY Ten quid says it will.

KATRINA I don't want to hear what noise it makes. Our aim is to stop it ever being built, if possible. *(Beat)* But if we don't, all right, ten quid.

Scene Seven

Ext. force field perimeter.

Effects: sound of construction. Clanky noises of metal things being slotted together.

ULJABAAN Is all proceeding to schedule?

MINION *(alien not exactly)*

ULJABAAN What's the problem?

MINION *(alien explanation)*

ULJABAAN Then you must be assembling it wrong. What did the instructions say to do?

MINION *(alien er...)*

ULJABAAN You didn't read the instructions, did you? You just ploughed on regardless.

MINION *(alien excuse)*

ULJABAAN Well clearly it wasn't as self-explanatory as it seemed, was it? This is a highly advanced piece of technology, you can't just guess how it fits together.

Effects: **ULJABAAN** *hands them the instructions.*

Here are the instructions. You are to follow them to the letter.

MINION *(alien question)*

ULJABAAN Why do you need an allen key? Wasn't there one inside the pack?

MINION *(alien yes, but...)*

ULJABAAN No, I'm not giving you a sonic allen key, you can make do with that one.

Scene Eight

Ext. disused well.

Effects: **MARGARET** *makes her way up a shallow incline.*

MARGARET *(calls)* Keith? Are you still down there?

Effects: **KEITH** *(thirties, pub bore type) is down the well.*

KEITH Hello? Is that you, Margaret?

MARGARET Yes.

KEITH Oh thank God. Hurry up and let me out!

MARGARET I'm not here to let you out, as such.

KEITH What?

MARGARET Mr Uljabaan asked me to check up on you. *(Beat)* How are you?

KEITH I've been down a well for three days! Down a well, no less!

MARGARET It's a dried-up well, Keith. It's not like you're sitting in two feet of cold water.

KEITH Is that meant to make me feel better?

MARGARET I can tip some cold water down there and you can see if you feel worse.

KEITH This is an outrage, you realise. An outrage.

MARGARET *(beat)* Is it, though?

KEITH I was laissez-faire about the aliens, very much laissez-faire. I was minding my own business, then with no warning, they sent me down here at gunpoint and took the ladder away!

MARGARET "Minding your own business"? That's a rather delicate euphemism for urinating up the side of their spaceship, isn't it?

KEITH I was on my way back from the pub. Better out than in.

MARGARET Your house was twenty seconds' walk away. Would it not have been better in for another twenty seconds?

KEITH Well—

MARGARET No, Keith, don't answer that. Because this is something of a habit with you. Everyone knows that.

KEITH *(beat)* Hm.

MARGARET There's not a lot of sympathy for you down in the village, you know.

KEITH Isn't there?

MARGARET I don't think anyone has said it's actually a shame you're trapped down a well.

KEITH Oh.

MARGARET I'm sending over a few visitors this afternoon. Some other residents you might like to apologise to.

KEITH And then will the aliens let me go?

MARGARET I'm afraid that's not up to me. But I could put in a good word for you.

KEITH Thanks.

MARGARET I'm sending you a bottle of water down in a bucket.

KEITH Can I send you a bottle back up?

MARGARET An empty bottle?

KEITH No, it's not empty, I've been using it as a *(beat)* bottle for keeping Lucozade in.

MARGARET No, you may not.

Scene Nine

Int. **LYONS** *house (study).*

Effects: **KATRINA** *and* **LUCY** *typing on laptop.*

LUCY So where are we going to hide this message in the newsletter? Are we going to write it really, really small and put it on the bottom?

KATRINA I think we can hide it better than that.

LUCY *(beat)* Yeah. Yeah, I know what you're thinking. Really, really small, on the bottom...and upside down.

KATRINA No. We want to hide it well so that if Uljabaan sees one of the newsletters, he won't think anything's amiss. So you know where we'll hide it?

LUCY Where?

KATRINA In the crossword.

LUCY Wow. *(Beat)* The newsletter doesn't have a crossword.

KATRINA I'm editing it this week, so if I want it to have a crossword, it can have a crossword.

LUCY So how do you hide it in the crossword?

KATRINA You make all the answers parts of a sentence which, when you put them together, makes up the message.

LUCY But how will whoever finds the newsletter know they're supposed to do the crossword to find a secret message? And how will they know to put all the words together to get the message? And what if they're rubbish at doing crosswords?

KATRINA *(beat)* They do it in Cold War films, it always works then. All right, we won't put it in the crossword.

LUCY Why don't we delete the poem in Mrs Winterton's Poetry Corner and put the message there?

KATRINA Of course! Nobody in the village would ever read that, because they've met her. OK, the second part of the plan: how do we get it outside?

LUCY We cover a copy of the newsletter in Pritt Stick and leave it next to the force field at the place where the Geonin are going in and out.

KATRINA Why Pritt Stick?

LUCY Because it sticks things for a bit and then they fall off. So one of the Geonin walks through, it sticks to his foot and falls off on the other side.

KATRINA This all seems a bit shonky, don't you think? Even without relying on the precise length of time a dab of semi-dried-out child's craft glue will stick a folded sheet of A4 to the foot of a hairy alien, we're relying on someone out there finding the newsletter and noticing the message.

LUCY The outside world has forgotten that Cresdon Green exists, though – so it might even be enough for them to just see the name of the newsletter. They'll go, "what? Cresdon Green? Where's that?" and then they'll investigate.

KATRINA But they might just think we're a fictional village, created for a science fiction programme.

LUCY Why would someone make a parish newsletter about a fictional village from a science fiction programme?

KATRINA Science fiction fans are weird, they do that sort of thing. *(Beat)* What the hell. Let's print this thing and go for it.

Effects: the newsletter starts printing off.

Scene Ten

Int. LYONS *house (living room).*

Effects: RICHARD *in armchair, listening to cricket on earphones. Door opens.* MARGARET *enters.*

MARGARET Richard? *(Beat)* Richard, please take your headphones off.

Effects: pause, then she claps her hands in front of his face, startling him.

Richard!

Effects: RICHARD *removes the headphones: he's listening to Test Match Special.*

RICHARD Sorry, I didn't hear you come in – I had my headphones on.

MARGARET What are you listening to?

RICHARD Test Match Special.

MARGARET How can you? There's no radio reception.

RICHARD It's one of my old tapes. Hedingley '91 against the Windies. Could you pass me the next one? It's marked "Tape seven of nineteen."

MARGARET Have you assembled the newsletters?

RICHARD Have I assembled the newsletters.

MARGARET Yes. Have you assembled the newsletters?

RICHARD I think I can answer your question more fully if I—

MARGARET You're sitting on them.

RICHARD Oh! So I am. I didn't see them there.

MARGARET But surely you put them there.

RICHARD *(beat)* I did. But I didn't *see* them there.

Effects: **MARGARET** *pulls the newsletters out from under* **RICHARD**.

MARGARET Thank you.

RICHARD It was no trouble.

MARGARET Good! Now you've got the hang of it, you can do it again next week.

RICHARD Oh. Are you still going to be busy next week then?

MARGARET Yes, at this rate. I still haven't finished measuring the height, weight and shoe size of everyone in the village.

RICHARD What for?

MARGARET He did explain why, but I've forgotten. Something to do with a clinical trial, there's a control group and so on. In the meantime I'm having to pass my chores on to other people – Madeleine's overseeing the allocation of table space in the village fête.

RICHARD What? Not after the bust-up she had with Penny over the charity shop rotas. She'll try to get her own back.

MARGARET They've had a bust-up? Why did no one tell me?

RICHARD You always know these things.

MARGARET I've been busy!

Effects: door opens. It's **GRAHAM**.

GRAHAM Margaret! It's all kicking off at the fête table allocation meeting!

MARGARET Coming! *(To herself)* Where's my laser pistol?

RICHARD Since when have you had a laser pistol?

Effects: she picks it up and checks the settings.

MARGARET It's just a small one, to speed things up by stopping people from arguing with me... *(Tuts)* I've forgotten to charge it up again.

Scene Eleven

Ext. bushes.

Effects: **KATRINA** *and* **LUCY** *are still waiting. A* **MINION** *is approaching.*

KATRINA *(low)* Go on, big fella. Go on.

LUCY *(low)* He's going to stand on this one.

KATRINA *(low)* Don't look down, just keep walking, keep walking...

Effects: the **MINION** *stands on the newsletter. It rustles.*

(Low) Yes!

LUCY *(low)* Get in!

Effects: the **MINION** *stops walking.*

MINION *(offstage)* Ruuuh?

KATRINA *(low)* Damn! He's seen it.

Effects: the **MINION** *starts shaking his foot around, making frustrated noises.*

LUCY *(low)* He's trying to shake it off.

Effects: MINION *shakes his foot harder, falls over.*

He fell on his arse!

KATRINA *(low)* Sh. I know it's funny, but sh.

Effects: the MINION *stands, acts casual, walks over to the force field, opens it up.*

LUCY *(low)* Are we going to give up now?

KATRINA *(low)* I don't know, maybe we should – wait.

LUCY *(low)* What?

KATRINA *(low)* He's dropped something.

Effects: the force field closes behind the MINION.

He's gone. Quick, let's grab it.

Effects: KATRINA *and* LUCY *leave the bushes, pick up a booklet.*

Oh my God.

LUCY What is it?

KATRINA It's the instructions for the thing they're building. Look.

LUCY Oh my God.

KATRINA No wonder Uljabaan hasn't been telling everyone what it is. Wait until Mum sees this!

Scene Twelve

Int. LYONS *house.*

Effects: MARGARET *struggles inside with a heavy can of petrol.* KATRINA *rushes to meet her.*

Mum! You've got to see this – why have you got a huge can full of petrol?

MARGARET Don't ask silly questions.

Effects: **MARGARET** *puts it down.*

I'm very busy, dear, so if you don't mind—

KATRINA No, Mum – look at this.

MARGARET Aren't you a bit old for comics?

KATRINA It's not a comic. It's the instruction manual for this thing Uljabaan's building.

MARGARET You stole it?

KATRINA No, I found it. You don't know what he's building, do you?

MARGARET No.

KATRINA The instructions are all in their language, but the pictures are pretty clear...let's skip to the last stage.

Effects: **KATRINA** *turns the pages of the booklet.*

MARGARET *(beat)* But this is monstrous.

KATRINA I thought you'd say that.

MARGARET Disgraceful.

KATRINA And that.

MARGARET He's building...a *wind turbine*?

KATRINA Apparently so.

MARGARET Right next to the village?

KATRINA Right next to the village.

MARGARET Doesn't he know that I spent two years challenging a decision to build a turbine in exactly that spot? And won?

KATRINA I think he probably does know that. I think that's why he's been keeping you busy, so you don't find out until it's too late.

MARGARET Well he has *got* to be stopped.

KATRINA Then we agree.

MARGARET I thought you were in favour of these ugly, noisy things?

KATRINA Only when humans are building them.

Scene Thirteen

Int. LYONS *house (study).*

Effects: **RICHARD** *is writing his novel again. Interior monologue.*

RICHARD Koeman leapt from the bridge onto the roof of the tram. "Give it up, Van Leutyens!" he shouted at the tall murderer who stood on the other side of the bendy bit they have in the middle of trams so they can go round corners. "For you, this tram is terminating early – and not due to planned engineering works!"

Effects: **KATRINA** *and* **MARGARET** *enter.*

MARGARET We need the computer.

RICHARD I'm just getting to the exciting bit.

KATRINA We also need your help with some flat-pack instructions.

RICHARD Ooh.

Effects: **KATRINA** *opens the instructions.*

KATRINA Here.

RICHARD Gosh. This looks even more complicated than that corner shelving unit I put up. Might even be a two-man job.

MARGARET We're not building it. We're going to scan it, and make a couple of little changes…

Scene Fourteen

Int. **ULJABAAN***'s house.*

Effects: **ULJABAAN** *is rifling through paperwork.*

ULJABAAN I can't believe that in your entire databank you don't have a copy of these instructions.

COMPUTER I'm not allowed to scan it, it's copyrighted.

ULJABAAN We're two thousand light years from Geosis, who's going to know? *(Tuts)* It's not here. It's not bloody here.

Effects: **MARGARET** *enters.*

MARGARET Not interrupting anything, am I?

ULJABAAN Margaret! Not at all – one of the minions has mislaid...a document. Just some dull paperwork, but if you do find it, I'd appreciate it if you could get it back to me. I shouldn't bother reading it, unless you're having trouble sleeping! Haha!

MARGARET Is this what you've been looking for?

ULJABAAN *(beat)* Oh. Yes, I'll just—

Effects: he takes it from her, tosses it in a corner.

Lob it into a corner, not really important, I'll deal with it later. *(Beat)* Did you read it?

MARGARET No, it was all written in Genoese or whatever you call it.

ULJABAAN Oh good! Just because I didn't want you to be bored, or whatever.

MARGARET Right. Well, here's the report you asked for on Patrick Naughton.

ULJABAAN Ah, Weird Patrick. What's your verdict?

MARGARET You were right, in as much as he *is* building a tank in his shed with a view to launching a full-on assault on your house.

ULJABAAN Right.

MARGARET However, the tank is made entirely from bits of old lawnmowers and sheets of MDF, apart from the cannon which is cannibalised from a pinball machine.

ULJABAAN Hmm. We'll give it a threat level of "medium", just to be on the safe side. Thank you.

MARGARET Glad I could help. Look at the time! I should get on.

Effects: she leaves. **ULJABAAN** *scrabbles for the instructions.*

ULJABAAN Give this to the minions and tell them to get cracking. We need this project back on schedule.

COMPUTER Will do.

ULJABAAN And hang up on that call to the homeworld, it must be costing a fortune.

Scene Fifteen

Ext. force field perimeter.

Effects: work still proceeding on the turbine.

ULJABAAN Is the assembly complete?

MINION *(gutteral alien language)*

ULJABAAN Very good. Now, everyone grab the rope and pull it upright. Pull!

Effects: **MINIONS** *pull.*

Pull!

Effects: **MINIONS** *pull.*

Pull!

Effects: **MINIONS** *pull. They keep pulling while he talks.*

Do you think it's helping, my shouting "Pull"? I think it's helping. *(Shouts)* Pull!

Effects: **MINIONS** *pull. The turbine is in position.*

Hm. It's smaller than I expected.

MINION *(gutteral alien language)*

ULJABAAN No, nobody in the outside world will be able to see it. It's covered by the same perception filter as the village, so only we in the village can see it.

MINION *(gutteral alien language)*

ULJABAAN Yes, the perception filter works on birds too. Why?

MINION *(gutteral alien language)*

ULJABAAN I suppose there is a chance they might fly into it and be killed, yes.

MINION *(sad alien mutter)*

ULJABAAN You like the birdies.

MINION *(sad alien yes)*

ULJABAAN Then we'll put a sign near it saying "BIRDIES KEEP AWAY".

MINION *(alien question?)*

ULJABAAN Of course birds can read. Any creature who's clever enough to migrate thousands of miles with perfect accuracy must be able to read. Right – very good chaps, back to the village.

MINION *(alien question?)*

ULJABAAN What do you mean, you've got some bits left over?

MINION *(look, here)*

ULJABAAN Oh. There are always a couple of bits left over when you've finished, aren't there. They're probably spares.

MINION *(so?)*

ULJABAAN Take them back to the spaceship and put them in the bottom drawer.

Scene Sixteen

Ext. disused well.

Effects: a crowd has gathered to look at the new thing.

KEITH *(down well)* It's jolly nice of you all to come and see me.

MARGARET We're not here to see you, Keith.

KEITH *(down well)* No?

KATRINA No, we're here to see the new thing Uljabaan's built just outside the village. You get the best view from here.

ULJABAAN Ah yes. It's what we call a Climate Extractor Whirligig.

MARGARET It's what we call a wind turbine.

ULJABAAN What? No no no. It's quite different.

KATRINA What does it do then?

ULJABAAN Well, it...sort of...turns round...

KATRINA And generates electricity?

ULJABAAN If you want to be simplistic about it. But it's capable of producing more than fifteen times the amount of energy your Earth devices are capable of, serving all our energy needs for the operation on your planet as it gathers pace. It's an altogether more advanced piece of technology—

MARGARET That looks exactly like a wind turbine.

Effects: soft whump whump whump in distance.

KATRINA Seems to be working. Easy to put together, was it?

ULJABAAN Yes.

KATRINA All straightforward.

ULJABAAN Yes.

KATRINA No bits left over.

ULJABAAN *(beat)* There's always some bits left over.

MARGARET I'm sure they weren't anything important. Not if your chaps followed the instructions.

ULJABAAN They absolutely did follow the instructions. I was very clear about that.

Effects: turbine creaks.

I expect they're supposed to make that creaking noise, aren't they.

Effects: buckle and creeeeeaaaak...

KATRINA Yes, and I expect they're supposed to sort of...slowly fall over.

GRAHAM Er...it's falling this way.

ULJABAAN But when it hits the force field, it'll—

Effects: massive fzzzzzz!

KATRINA Disintegrate?

ULJABAAN You were behind this.

KATRINA Yes, obviously.

MARGARET With a little help.

ULJABAAN *(beat)* I see. You think my plans can be hindered so easily?

KATRINA Yes.

ULJABAAN You're wrong. I shall simply build another, bigger and [better than –]

MINION *(alien interruption)*

ULJABAAN Really? I didn't realise the budget was that tight. Then we shall build another that is not bigger and better, but is in every respect identical to the one that just—

MINION *(alien interruption)*

ULJABAAN Oh. Then we shall build another that is slightly smaller and almost as good, which nevertheless will—

MINION *(alien interruption)*

ULJABAAN Oh for heaven's sake. What can we afford?

MINION *(alien interruption)*

ULJABAAN I see. Then we shall take Keith out of the well and force him to generate electricity on an exercise bike!

Effects: crowd cheers.

End of Episode 1.3

WELCOME TO OUR VILLAGE, PLEASE INVADE CAREFULLY

Episode 1.4 – "Little Green Lights"

WELCOME TO
OUR VILLAGE
PLEASE INVADE
CAREFULLY

Scene One

Int. ULJABAAN's *house.*

Effects: MARGARET *and* RICHARD *are having tea with* ULJABAAN.

ULJABAAN I'm sure you're wondering why I invited you here today.

MARGARET *(beat)* No. Were you, Richard?

RICHARD No. People often invite Margaret and I over to their houses for tea, I didn't feel I was being kept in the dark about anything.

ULJABAAN Nevertheless, I would like to segue the conversation into explaining why I invited you here today.

MARGARET Would it help if I asked why you invited us here today?

ULJABAAN It would, thank you.

MARGARET Why did you invite us here today, Mr Uljabaan?

ULJABAAN Well, I'm preparing for a visit from my immediate superior. His name is Gryvook.

MARGARET He sounds nice.

ULJABAAN He isn't. He's...quite mean. And he's coming to assess the pilot scheme, see how our little mini-invasion of your village is going and, fingers crossed, give us the go-ahead for the full invasion of Earth.

RICHARD *(unconvincingly)* Er, yes. Fingers crossed.

ULJABAAN Thing is, the invasions programme is undergoing a series of cutbacks. Our master strategists had predicted by now we'd be winning the war against our mortal enemies the Thoufron.

RICHARD The Few-thron?

MARGARET No, the Throuvon.

ULJABAAN No no – Thoufron. I know, it's a silly name. Anyway, it's a real drain on the old coffers, fighting a war on eighty-nine fronts, so I need to present a compelling fiscal case for conquering this planet. And I'd like you to help me, Richard.

MARGARET That sounds right up your street.

RICHARD Does it? I usually specialise in VAT returns.

MARGARET I can't imagine that budgeting for a global invasion is much more complicated than a VAT return.

ULJABAAN I'd appreciate it. By law, we have to use an independent financial assessor, it can't be anyone from our own planet.

RICHARD Couldn't you get someone from one of those other planets you've invaded?

ULJABAAN Most of them can't count. Many are gaseous wraithlike creatures with no fingers, and a surprising amount of the others are giant mice.

MARGARET Go on, Richard.

RICHARD *(reluctantly)* All right.

ULJABAAN Splendid! I've printed the accounts for you here...

Effects: Thud.

RICHARD *(beat)* Yes.

ULJABAAN You can use my study. Please don't talk to the printer yourself, he's been spreading all sorts of malicious gossip about me.

RICHARD Righto.

Effects: **RICHARD** *leaves the room.*

ULJABAAN And Margaret, there's a matter I need your help with.

MARGARET What?

ULJABAAN *(beat)* You're not going to like it.

Scene Two

Int. cricket pavilion.

Effects: daytime. **KATRINA** *and* **LUCY** *are having a meeting.*

KATRINA This meeting of the Cresdon Green Resistance Group will now come to order.

LUCY I thought it already had.

KATRINA No, I haven't called out everyone's name yet. Katrina Lyons – here. Lucy Alexander?

LUCY Yeah.

KATRINA Weird Patrick?

Nothing.

So, he meant it when he said he was never coming back.

LUCY It was an accident. I didn't mean to break his stupid Xena Warrior Princess mug.

KATRINA I know he's annoying but we need all the help we can get. I was planning a brainstorming session today.

LUCY "Brainstorming session"? Excuse me, I didn't realise we were in the office of, like, a corporate banking society.

KATRINA *(beat)* What does that even mean?

LUCY I'm just saying, God, you're making it like work.

KATRINA Achieving anything worthwhile is hard work. I bet the French resistance wasn't as exciting as it is in films. Or as whimsical as it was in *'Allo 'Allo*.

LUCY What's *'Allo 'Allo*?

KATRINA You need never know.

LUCY The resistance thing was exciting at the beginning. But I'm sort of over it now.

KATRINA You're "over" it? You're "over" trying to prevent humanity becoming subservient to an alien menace?

LUCY It's impossible though. They've got laser guns and a spaceship and a really, really clever computer, and we've got...

KATRINA We've got wit. Ingenuity. Pluck. Heart. Soul. Guts... *(Beat)* ...Legs. Lots of things.

LUCY But not laser guns. Or any guns.

KATRINA We don't need guns! I'll think of something. I'll come up with a new plan that will definitely...well, not *definitely* work, there's a lot you can't legislate for. It will *probably*... All right, it will look plausible. And while I'm doing that—

Effects: pieces of mug put on table.

You try to glue Patrick's mug back together.

LUCY Aw.

Scene Three

Int. ULJABAAN*'s house.*

Effects: ULJABAAN *still talking to* MARGARET.

ULJABAAN You really can't think of anyone?

MARGARET No, I don't think anyone in *this* village will consent to their child being slaughtered, roasted and served at a banquet.

ULJABAAN How sure are you of that? Eighty per cent?

MARGARET Why do you need to do this?

ULJABAAN I'm afraid it's a longstanding Geonin tradition. When you're the first colonists on a planet, you're supposed to serve up a roasted native child when your commanding officer arrives.

If someone was willing to offer up their child as a...tasty sacrifice, there would be substantial benefits for them.

MARGARET What possible compensation could you offer for giving up their child to be eaten by aliens?

ULJABAAN *(pause)* After the invasion, they can have an island.

MARGARET An island.

ULJABAAN A really big one, like Japan.

MARGARET But would Japan compensate for the lingering feelings of loss and guilt and regret?

ULJABAAN It's a very beautiful country, and the transport network is first class.

MARGARET But no, it wouldn't.

ULJABAAN No. I wish I didn't have to do this. Maybe I'm just being paranoid, but I feel like slaughtering one of their children for food might sour the villagers' opinion of me.

MARGARET Look, I might be able to help.

ULJABAAN Oh thank you. Katrina is a little older than I wanted, but it would kill two birds with one stone.

MARGARET No, not Katrina.

ULJABAAN Why not?

MARGARET Because she's my daughter and I love her.

ULJABAAN Do you? I didn't realise.

Scene Four

Int. LYONS *house (kitchen).*

Effects: MARGARET *working in the kitchen.* KATRINA *enters.*

KATRINA Mum, what are you doing with all that mince?

MARGARET I'm trying to get it to look...sort of...child-shaped.

KATRINA *(beat)* I'm trying to decide whether to say "Good grief, why?" or to tell you it doesn't.

MARGARET That side's not finished yet. Look at it from this side.

Effects: KATRINA *walks round.*

KATRINA From this side it looks like Peppa Pig.

MARGARET Oh, fiddle.

Effects: **MARGARET** *throws mince down on the table.*

KATRINA Right, *now* I'm going to say "Good grief, why?"

MARGARET I'm making it for Mr Uljabaan.

KATRINA Because...he can't have a child of his own?

MARGARET He needs it for a banquet. It's one of their traditions.

KATRINA What a hideous bunch.

MARGARET Aren't you always the one preaching "cultural sensitivity"?

KATRINA I'm fairly comfortable with being insensitive to a man who likes eating meat effigies of children.

MARGARET He doesn't like it. In fact, the tradition is normally to eat an actual child—

KATRINA But he's allergic to human flesh?

MARGARET no, he just isn't comfortable about the whole business, even though he needs to make a good impression on his commanding officer.

KATRINA His commanding officer's visiting?

MARGARET Yes, for an assessment.

KATRINA And will his boss be all right with not getting a real human child?

MARGARET He'll be perfectly all right with it because we're not going to tell him. How does he know we don't taste like ground beef? Now please get out of my kitchen so I can get on.

KATRINA I could help.

MARGARET Cookery is hardly your forté.

KATRINA No, but I did sculpture at school.

MARGARET With meat?

KATRINA Yes. It was the nineties, we were all trying to be Damian Hirst. Mine had gone a bit rancid before the end-of-year exhibition, but if anything that underlined the symbolism of the piece, so I thought it was very unfair of them to give me a "C" just because it smelled a bit.

Scene Five

Int. ULJABAAN's *house.*

Effects: RICHARD *talking to* ULJABAAN.

RICHARD The final cost will depend on how easily you subdue the global population.

ULJABAAN Indeed.

RICHARD If humanity just surrenders, then the overall cost could be as little as this...

Effects: RICHARD *hands* ULJABAAN *a piece of paper.*

ULJABAAN *(pleasantly surprised)* Oh. There might even be enough money left over to invade that inhabited moon of Jupiter.

RICHARD There's an inhabited moon of Jupiter?

ULJABAAN Just a small amount of aquatic life. I say invasion, it'd be more of a fishing trip really. But this is good news!

RICHARD Ah, but if there's a lot of resistance, running guerilla battles and so on, it could be as much as...

Effects: hands ULJABAAN *another piece of paper.*

ULJABAAN *(unpleasantly surprised)* Oh. If that's the cost, they'll either tell me to abandon the invasion plan...

RICHARD *(encouraged)* Right.

ULJABAAN Or just fry all living matter on the planet.

RICHARD *(beat)* I'd rather you didn't.

ULJABAAN Me neither, but it's cheap and we can still extract the mineral wealth afterwards.

RICHARD But if you keep us alive, you could...turn Earth into a manufacturing base.

ULJABAAN I'm afraid our manufacturing is all mechanised... *(Clicks fingers)* But we're always having trouble finding staff for our operations hub.

RICHARD That sounds important.

ULJABAAN It is. When the Geonin citizenry need to raise issues with central command, they're directed towards the operations hub where their comments are logged, responded to, and passed up the chain.

RICHARD It sounds like a call centre.

ULJABAAN Yes! That's what you call them – a call centre. We can set up a subspace communications link between Earth and Geosis and turn your planet into an enormous call centre. Great idea, Richard.

RICHARD It wasn't *exactly* my idea.

ULJABAAN There's no need for modesty. You deserve the credit and I want you to help me present this plan to the supreme commander.

RICHARD Oh...good.

Scene Six

Int. **LYONS** *house (kitchen).*

Effects: **KATRINA** *and* **MARGARET** *still working on the meat child.*

KATRINA These chipolatas are much bigger than a child's fingers, surely.

MARGARET They're all we've got. Look—

Effects: sausage chop.

Cut them in half like so, and then we just say he was obese.

KATRINA Hmm. I suppose that has its own internal logic, that we killed the fleshiest child we could find.

MARGARET Exactly. Bulk him out, slap some more mince on the top.

KATRINA All right, but please stop calling it "him".

Effects: slap of mince. **RICHARD** *walks in.*

MARGARET How did it go?

RICHARD *(beat)* Mixed.

KATRINA What was mixed?

MARGARET He's been helping Uljabaan with the invasion budget.

KATRINA Oh, Dad.

RICHARD Your mother badgered me into it.

MARGARET You should be getting into his good books, if he's going to be in charge of everything.

RICHARD Yes… I would rather he wasn't though.

MARGARET I don't know. We're short supply of strong, decisive leadership these days.

RICHARD He may well destroy us all from space. Is that strong and decisive enough for you?

KATRINA He's going to do that?

RICHARD It came up during the meeting.

MARGARET How did you manage to annoy him that much in one afternoon?

RICHARD Not because I annoyed him, because it's cheaper. But although it's still an option, I think I've managed to steer him away from it.

MARGARET Well done. They might erect a statue of you for that. Or at least name the stand behind the goal in a football stadium after you.

RICHARD The bad news is that I seem to have inadvertently steered him towards turning Earth into a giant outsourced call centre for their empire.

KATRINA Oh.

MARGARET It's a step up from being dead.

KATRINA I can tell you've never worked in a call centre.

Scene Seven

Int. ULJABAAN's *house.*

Effects: ULJABAAN *talking to the* COMPUTER.

ULJABAAN Computer?

COMPUTER Yes, sir?

ULJABAAN Give me a haircut.

COMPUTER Certainly. What are we doing with it today?

ULJABAAN Cutting it.

COMPUTER Have you considered making your fringe into more of a feature?

ULJABAAN Could you please just— *(beat)* what, you mean brushed over to one side and sort of hanging just above one eye?

COMPUTER Or all the way down to your chin like Phil Oakey from The Human League.

ULJABAAN Who are The Human League? Another resistance group?

COMPUTER No, they were more electro-pop.

ULJABAAN This isn't the day for reckless experimentation. I need to look absolutely professional. So just give me the usual.

COMPUTER Stand still and I'll lower the Haircut 100 into position.

Effects: a device lowers itself onto ULJABAAN's *head. Then, the sound of rapid haircutting.*

ULJABAAN Are the minions all groomed?

COMPUTER Yes, and their claws have been manicured.

ULJABAAN Has the spaceship been cleaned?

COMPUTER Yes.

ULJABAAN Is the banquet ready?

COMPUTER *(beat)* As ready as it'll ever be.

Effects: haircut finishes, haircut machine rises.

ULJABAAN How do I look?

COMPUTER I still think you should have gone for the fringe.

ULJABAAN There's no time. I need to see Richard and go over his presentation, we should be [able to –]

COMPUTER Alert. A shuttle is arriving from orbit.

ULJABAAN But he's not supposed to arrive for another hour.

COMPUTER Yes. My analysis indicates that he is a bit early.

Effects: ULJABAAN *runs from the room.*

Scene Eight

Ext. village green.

Effects: a spaceship lands. Door opens, GRYVOOK *emerges.*

ULJABAAN Supreme commander Gryvook, welcome to—

GRYVOOK Oh God, it stinks.

ULJABAAN *(beat)* I hadn't noticed. Your human guise suits you well.

GRYVOOK Does it? It's itching me. I was tempted not to bother with it but, you know, tradition and all that.

ULJABAAN Of course. Tradition. It's so important, isn't it. Did you have a good journey?

GRYVOOK I've no idea. I was in suspended animation. But I've arrived on time and alive, so I presume it was fine.

ULJABAAN Good.

GRYVOOK At least I managed to find a parking space. Last place I went to, the native population had covered ninety-eight per cent of the land mass with enormous metal spikes, for some reason. Had to land in the sea. Which was made of acid. Ruined the finish on the ship.

ULJABAAN Well, our native population haven't quite built over every inch of available space yet.

GRYVOOK Is that the native population there?

ULJABAAN Not all of them, there are another seven billion outside the force field, but—

GRYVOOK You're just letting them wander around unsupervised? You haven't even tagged them.

ULJABAAN I'm using subtler methods.

GRYVOOK Your generation and your "modern" invasion techniques. I bet you haven't even killed anyone yet as an example to the rest, have you?

ULJABAAN I haven't had cause to do so.

GRYVOOK You haven't had the balls to do so, you mean.

ULJABAAN With respect, sir, for the purposes of my research programme it's best if the natives can operate in relative normality.

GRYVOOK Yes, yes, we'll discuss business over dinner. I hope it's a *traditional* banquet?

ULJABAAN It's all so traditional you'll think I'm your mother in disguise.

GRYVOOK *(beat)* You're not, are you?

ULJABAAN No.

GRYVOOK Oh good. Because she has tried to catch me out like that before.

Scene Nine

Int. **ULJABAAN**'s *house.*

Effects: **ULJABAAN** *walks in, followed by* **GRYVOOK**.

ULJABAAN Um...ta-dah.

GRYVOOK Not a bad spread.

Effects: they sit down. **LUCY** *walks over.*

LUCY My name's Lucy, I'll be your waitress this afternoon.

ULJABAAN What are you doing here?

LUCY Mrs L asked me to help out, seeing as I'm the only one in the village with waitressing experience.

ULJABAAN You have waitressing experience?

LUCY I worked at Razzle Dazzle Pizza for three days and oh my God it was the longest three days of my life. The manager, right, was this total bitch who docked our pay for every minute we were late and then one morning she was an *hour* late but we didn't get to dock *her* pay and when we had a meal break you were allowed three toppings on your pizza which sounds alright until you find out cheese and tomato count as two of your three—

GRYVOOK The youngling is making a noise, Uljabaan.

ULJABAAN Miss Alexander, your grievances with the manageress of the Aylesbury branch of Razzle Dazzle Pizza are noted, now kindly do the job you were brought here to do.

LUCY All right, all right...our special today, sir, is a roasted human child served in a whiskey cream sauce, with seasonal vegetables and potatoes dauphinoise.

Effects: **LUCY** *serves up.*

GRYVOOK I'm quite impressed, Uljabaan.

ULJABAAN Wait until you see what's for dessert. An ingenious local delicacy known as Fruit Corners.

GRYVOOK Explain more.

ULJABAAN A plastic tray, containing a portion of fermented milk. But! The corner of the tray houses a smaller portion of compacted fruit. Before eating, one stirs the compacted fruit into the fermented milk.

GRYVOOK Why must they be kept apart until the moment of eating?

ULJABAAN That, I've never asked. I assume that, when mixed, they become volatile, and so must be transported separately.

GRYVOOK Makes sense.

Effects: sudden commotion as **KATRINA** *bursts in.*

KATRINA Stop!

ULJABAAN How did you get past my guards?

KATRINA I knocked on the front door and before they answered, I ran round the back and let myself in.

GRYVOOK Who is she?

ULJABAAN Her name's Katrina Lyons. She's...annoying.

GRYVOOK Kill her.

KATRINA Wait! Before you kill me, hear me out.

GRYVOOK No.

KATRINA Yes.

GRYVOOK No.

KATRINA Yes.

GRYVOOK Shut up.

KATRINA Stop being so rude.

GRYVOOK I'm not interested in anything inferior life forms have to say.

KATRINA But I've got something to tell you that will shock you to your very core.

GRYVOOK Why would I want to be shocked to my very core? That doesn't sound pleasant at all.

KATRINA It's something you urgently need to know.

GRYVOOK *(sighs)* Go on then.

KATRINA That meat you're eating...is actually *not* human flesh.

LUCY *(gasps)* No.

KATRINA You already knew that.

LUCY Oh yeah.

GRYVOOK So, Uljabaan. A "traditional" greeting banquet, eh?

ULJABAAN I can explain.

GRYVOOK I must've been to at least thirty of these bloody banquets down the years. And the meat has always been... awful. Gristly, stringy, fatty, flavourless...poisonous, in one case. But this is delicious. What is it?

KATRINA *(deflated)* Beef mince slapped over some chicken breasts, with sausages and black pudding used for the limbs, and it's all wrapped in parma ham.

ULJABAAN What did you make the fingernails from?

KATRINA Celery.

LUCY Ugh, I ate one of those. I *hate* celery.

KATRINA Was this before or after you forgot it wasn't really a human child?

LUCY *(beat)* I, er...can't remember now.

GRYVOOK What did you hope to gain from revealing this, Miss Lyons?

KATRINA I wanted you to be pissed off with Uljabaan so you'd cancel the invasion of Earth.

GRYVOOK *(to* **ULJABAAN***)* I thought you had it all under control?

ULJABAAN These two are the only ones offering resistance. And it's mostly her, she leads the youngling astray.

LUCY That's true, she does lead me astray.

KATRINA And I wasn't even meant to be here. It's lucky for humanity that I was, frankly.

GRYVOOK Put this one in the cells. I want to talk to her.

Effects: **MINION** *drags* **KATRINA** *away.*

KATRINA Don't worry, Lucy. I'll think of something!

LUCY Last time you said that, you came up with this plan.

KATRINA *(offstage)* Yes, fair point.

Scene Ten

Int. cells.

Effects: **RICHARD** *enters.*

MINION *(alien aggressive shout)*

RICHARD I, er, need to speak to the prisoner.

KATRINA *(offstage)* Dad!

RICHARD Uljabaan said it was fine.

MINION *(alien assent)*

RICHARD Thank you.

Effects: he walks over to **KATRINA***'s cell.*

KATRINA *(low)* Right. I'll pretend to be ill, then when he opens the cell, you whack him over the head.

RICHARD What?

KATRINA *(low)* You've come to help me escape, haven't you?

RICHARD No, I wanted a hand with my PowerPoint presentation. I've got this picture of the Earth and I want it to rotate.

KATRINA Then you'll need to find a rotating animation of the Earth and put it in there. Your laptop can't make a three-dimensional model out of a two-dimensional image.

RICHARD Why not?

KATRINA Because your laptop isn't magic, Dad.

MINION *(offstage; alien order)*

RICHARD Oh dear. Sounds like they're ready for me. If I can't convince him about the call centre thing, what do I do?

KATRINA Tell him we'd make great pets. Or gifts for that difficult-to-buy-for relative.

Scene Eleven

Int. **ULJABAAN**'s *house.*

Effects: **ULJABAAN** *and* **GRYVOOK** *finishing up their meal.*

GRYVOOK Very decent, field commander.

ULJABAAN I'm glad it measured up to your expectations.

GRYVOOK Although I'm concerned you seem to be picking up some of the humans' habits, like using napkins and wearing shoes. I hope you're not going native, field commander.

ULJABAAN No, I'm just engaging with them to better understand them. It's how I operate. I'm a people person.

GRYVOOK You're not a person.

ULJABAAN No, I know, I just meant – Computer, why aren't we getting on with the presentation?

COMPUTER I was waiting for you to—

ULJABAAN It was supposed to begin forty seconds ago. *(Claps hands)* Come on, bring Richard in.

COMPUTER All right. *(Calls)* Richard!

Effects: **RICHARD** *enters.*

RICHARD Did you manage to find me a globe that spins round?

COMPUTER Yes, and I can also make it bounce up and down like a basketball and then go through a hoop.

RICHARD Don't do that.

COMPUTER OK. Let me know if you change your mind.

GRYVOOK *(to* **ULJABAAN***)* Who is this, please?

ULJABAAN Richard Lyons, one of this planet's leading financial experts.

RICHARD Well, I wouldn't say—

ULJABAAN Don't keep the supreme commander waiting.

RICHARD Right. So. We've all been there. You invade a planet and suck out its mineral wealth, but then what do you do with the native population?

GRYVOOK Usually I hunt them for sport.

RICHARD Oh. Aha! But what if you could use them to save millions of pounds—

GRYVOOK What are "pounds"?

RICHARD Er, millions of units of your own native currency, each and every year?

GRYVOOK What is a "year"?

RICHARD *(beat)* What I'm trying to say is, this idea will save you money.

GRYVOOK Right. Carry on.

RICHARD The Earth contains more than five billion people of working age, most of whom are capable of being civil and performing clearly-prescribed tasks without being shouted at too much. Give them all a crash course in your native language, and hey presto!

GRYVOOK Who is Presto and why are you shouting at him? Is it just me or does this make no sense?

RICHARD And...there you go, you need never worry about your customer service needs again!

GRYVOOK *(beat)* You're suggesting we convert Earth into an outsourced communications hub for our empire?

ULJABAAN Yes. The resultant savings will more than cover the cost of the invasion.

GRYVOOK Hmm. As it happens we are looking at new options in that area.

ULJABAAN The Earth would be ideal. They love telephones here – even though I blocked off all communication with the outside world months ago, eighty-one per cent of the inhabitants still carry their phones around anyway. Occasionally I see one of them get his or her phone out and stroke the screen, sadly.

GRYVOOK I'll give it serious consideration. Excuse me, I'm going to get some air.

RICHARD I hope you enjoy your walk around our village.

GRYVOOK I'm not going for a walk, I'm going to get some air from my ship. I don't know how you can bear to breathe this stuff.

Effects: **GRYVOOK** *stands and leaves.*

Scene Twelve

Int. cell.

Effects: **GRYVOOK** *enters, breathing a la Darth Vader. Then he stops and says:*

GRYVOOK Oh, that's the stuff.

KATRINA What have you got there?

GRYVOOK It's a cannister of compressed air from the crystal spheres of Bouragella. Although I seem to have bought sparkling by mistake – I usually just get still. *(Sniffs)* Daxian?

MINION *(alien language)*

GRYVOOK Leave us, I want to talk to the prisoner.

Effects: **MINION** *shuffles away.*

(Beat) No, I meant leave the room, not just stand a bit further away.

Effects: **MINION** *shuffles out of room.*

And close the door.

Effects: door closes.

Now. Do you know how many worlds the Geonin have conquered?

KATRINA No.

GRYVOOK As of last week, three hundred and seventeen. Three hundred and forty-four if you count the worlds we've invaded twice.

KATRINA If you're so good, why'd you have to invade them twice?

GRYVOOK Because they were getting lippy, so we invaded them again just to show them. When we invade a planet, Miss Lyons, it knows it's been invaded.

KATRINA But do you really *want* to invade the Earth? We've used most of the mineral wealth.

GRYVOOK What for?

KATRINA Roads and cars, which save us from having to walk everywhere, and gyms, which we build because otherwise we don't get enough exercise. Massive shopping centres which everyone goes to even though they find them depressing. Planes, which we use to fly fruit around the world instead of eating the fruit which grows half a mile away. And of course guns and missiles and stuff for killing people.

GRYVOOK Killing each other?

KATRINA Yes, until now we hadn't found any other intelligent species to massacre so we've had to do it to each other.

GRYVOOK Right. But we do have plans to use the native population.

KATRINA Oh yes. I've got a picture on my phone of a typical example of the native population.

Effects: **KATRINA** *brings up a picture on her phone.*

What he's wearing there is the current Arsenal away shirt.

GRYVOOK What is "Arsenal"?

KATRINA A sports team.

GRYVOOK And he's a member of the team?

KATRINA No.

GRYVOOK Ah, then he's infiltrated them as a spy.

KATRINA No. He just likes wearing it.

GRYVOOK But it's disgusting. It's purple and black hoops with a red trim.

KATRINA I know. But they change it every year to sell men like him a new one, and they've done all the designs that look nice. So now they just throw colours together more or less at random. He paid forty-five pounds for it.

GRYVOOK Why do you have a photograph of him?

KATRINA He was, er, my boyfriend, briefly. But there you go, that's how stupid I am, too.

GRYVOOK Hmm. This changes things. Thank you, Ms Lyons – you may go.

KATRINA Great. *(Pause)* The, er, door's still locked?

GRYVOOK Oh.

> *Effects:* GRYVOOK *rattles the door of the cell.*

For heaven's sake. Daxian!

Scene Thirteen

> *Int.* LYONS *house.*

> *Effects:* KATRINA *enters.*

KATRINA Nailed it!

MARGARET Don't use filthy language in this house, Katrina.

KATRINA No, Mum, I think I might have put Uljabaan's boss off the Earth invasion for good.

RICHARD Oh.

KATRINA You don't have to look so crestfallen, Dad. You didn't want the Earth to be turned into a giant call centre.

RICHARD No, but... I'm a bit tired. I might go to bed.

Effects: **RICHARD** *slopes away upstairs.*

MARGARET Well, I hope you're happy.

KATRINA Yes, I am happy.

MARGARET Well, then good for you.

KATRINA You say that, but it somehow sounds like you don't mean it.

MARGARET He put a lot of work into this, Katrina. It's a bit insensitive of you to lord it over him.

KATRINA I wasn't lording it. This is just me being proud of something I've achieved. I realise it's unfamiliar.

MARGARET I'm going to bed too.

Effects: **MARGARET** *leaves the room.*

KATRINA Seriously, I've just saved the world! Is nobody even going to say "Well done"? It's not like I'm asking you to erect a statue of me, or name a stand behind the goal in a football ground after me. *(Beat)* Although that would be nice.

Scene Fourteen

Int. cricket pavilion.

Effects: champagne cork pops.

LUCY Woohoo!

KATRINA I told you my plan would work.

LUCY Your plan didn't work.

KATRINA We got the result we wanted.

LUCY Yeah, but not because of your plan. That backfired completely.

KATRINA Did Boudica have to put up with this sort of nit-picking when she drove the Romans out of Britain? "Er, technically I think you'll find it wasn't your idea to burn down Colchester, it just caught fire and you took advantage".

LUCY All right, it was all down to your brilliant plan. Can I have some champagne please?

KATRINA Not with your dad still taking violent revenge on anyone who gives you alcohol. You can have an Appletiser.

Effects: **KATRINA** *pours fizz into a glass.*

LUCY I don't even get a drink for helping you defeat an alien invasion?

KATRINA You can come up to London when you turn eighteen and I'll pay for you to get plastered.

LUCY Promise?

KATRINA Promise.

LUCY Then it was all worth it.

Effects: glasses clink. They drink. Knock at door.

It's open!

KATRINA *(hisses)* Lucy, we don't just let people into—

Effects: door opens, **ULJABAAN** *enters.*

ULJABAAN Ah! I thought I'd find you here.

KATRINA Yes, because...we're really into cricket now.

ULJABAAN You don't have to pretend, I know this is your headquarters.

LUCY How did you find out?

ULJABAAN I can see the cricket pavilion from my kitchen window. I've noticed you going in and out several times.

LUCY I told you we should've used my dad's greenhouse.

KATRINA But it's completely transparent.

LUCY Exactly. It's the last place they'd expect to see us.

KATRINA It doesn't matter now. Not now we've convinced your boss to give up on the invasion.

ULJABAAN You're mistaken. He's just communicating with the homeworld and then I'm confident he'll give us the go-ahead.

KATRINA We'll see.

ULJABAAN Yes, we will.

KATRINA *(beat)* When? It's just, I've opened this champagne and it'll go flat.

LUCY I'll help you drink it.

KATRINA No you won't. Uljabaan, will you have a glass?

ULJABAAN Yes.

Effects: **KATRINA** *pours him a glass.*

Thank you. To the Geonin conquest of the Earth!

KATRINA To...the exact opposite of that!

Effects: chink. Then the door opens and **GRYVOOK** *enters.*

GRYVOOK Here you are. Are you busy?

LUCY He's gloating at her, and she's gloating at him.

GRYVOOK Loath as I am to interrupt a good gloating session, I need to get on. I'll admit I was sceptical about your insistence on this research programme, Uljabaan, but you were quite right.

ULJABAAN I'm glad to hear you say so.

GRYVOOK These humans are a peculiar species. In fact, I'm baffled they haven't already wiped themselves out. So we've decided to delay our decision on the invasion for one Earth year so you can continue your research.

ULJABAAN What?

KATRINA What?

LUCY *(beat)* What?

ULJABAAN What about the call centre?

GRYVOOK Central command tell me they've resolved that problem. You know the planet Laxina C?

ULJABAAN The place where the native population has the power of precognition?

GRYVOOK That's the one. We conquered it last month.

KATRINA Surprised they didn't see it coming.

GRYVOOK We're outsourcing operations to there. It's ideal – they know what your problem is before you call, so they can offer the solution immediately. No, this is very important work you're doing here, and we mean to let you continue.

ULJABAAN *(sighs)* Seeing as how it's very important, can I have more resources?

GRYVOOK No. Anyway, if I set off now I can get back to the homeworld by the end of the next star cycle. Youngling!

LUCY I'm seventeen, you know.

GRYVOOK Did you put some of that meat in a doggy bag and leave it in my ship with a bottle of wine as requested?

LUCY Yes, sir.

GRYVOOK Excellent. *(Beat)* You didn't steal any of my air, did you?

LUCY *(offended)* No.

GRYVOOK Good.

Effects: **GRYVOOK** *strides out.*

LUCY He's a terrible tipper. All he left at the end of the meal were two small purple rocks.

ULJABAAN Those aren't rocks, those are extremely rare Mungnian gemstones.

LUCY Are they valuable?

ULJABAAN No.

LUCY What a git. I'm glad I stole some of his air.

ULJABAAN So, Miss Lyons. We have another year of this to look forward to.

KATRINA Might not be a year. We might get shot of you sooner than that.

ULJABAAN Please keep trying, it's all good material for the research programme.

KATRINA And just you keep on patronising us and underestimating us. One day we'll make you regret the day you picked a fight with the planet Earth, and send you home with your tail between your legs—

ULJABAAN We don't have tails.

KATRINA Figure of speech – and you'll have to go crawling back to your boss and admit that two ordinary, and yet also remarkable, human women outwitted you.

LUCY Yeah. One day.

Effects: **KATRINA** *and* **LUCY** *go to leave, then* **LUCY** *says:*

LUCY But in the meantime, please consider Lyons Quality Catering for your next event.

ULJABAAN I certainly will.

End of Episode 1.4

EFFECTS LIST

In the scripts, "Effects" is a catch-all term covering anything which wasn't clear from the dialogue. Some were provided live by the cast, some were played in. If you're performing the scripts on stage, many effects which we played in will be unnecessary (footsteps, for example). Accordingly, I've restricted this list to the effects you're likely to need.

Shop doorbell
Cash register
Alien computer noise
A recording of "Jerusalem"
Computer bleep
Printer waking up
Computer scanning noise
Computer display noise
Noises of pub attractions
Pub ambiance
Pub on fire
Burning pub collapses in on itself
Noise like a cross between a printer and a knitting machine
Sci-fi technology noise
Firework-type noises
Rapid burst of speeded-up cricket noise
Window being smashed
Cricket ball vapourised after hitting force field
Telephone babble
Computer running many things at once
Star Trek replicator-type noise
Cricket bat hitting a fence
Rumble of thunder
Rain
Computer woozily goes out of control
Computer explodes
Computer is switched on
Email-type "new message" noise
Cash register noise
Spaceship being hit by implements
Electronic handcuffs being released
Garden hoe wedged violently into printer

Cat meows and purrs
Siren
Villagers singing "Consider Yourself" from *Oliver!*
Construction noises
Radio cricket commentary
Force field opening and closing
Wind turbine hoisted into position
Turbine operating
Turbine creaking, buckling and falling over
Turbine disintegrating in force field
Haircutting machine working rapidly
Spaceship landing
Spaceship door opening

THIS IS NOT THE END

**Visit samuelfrench.co.uk
and discover the best
theatre bookshop
on the internet**

A vast range of plays
Acting and theatre books
Gifts

samuelfrench.co.uk

samuelfrenchltd

samuel french uk